Here Today
and
Gone Tomorrow

THE STORY OF WORLD'S FAIRS AND EXPOSITIONS

To Glenn
with my hope you'll enjoy
these trips to the fair!

Suzanne Hilton

Nov. 4, 1978

Here Today and Gone Tomorrow

THE STORY OF WORLD'S FAIRS AND EXPOSITIONS

by

Suzanne Hilton

THE WESTMINSTER PRESS

Philadelphia

BOOK DESIGN BY DOROTHY ALDEN SMITH

First edition

Published by The Westminster Press®
Philadelphia, Pennsylvania

PRINTED IN THE UNITED STATES OF AMERICA
9 8 7 6 5 4 3 2 1

Library of Congress Cataloging in Publication Data

Hilton, Suzanne.
  Here today and gone tomorrow.

  Bibliography: p.
  Includes index.
  SUMMARY: Presents accounts of eight large
expositions held in the United States from 1852 to
1964 that not only reflected but stimulated
technological progress.
  1. Exhibitions—Juvenile literature.
[1. Exhibitions] I. Title.
T395.H54   607'.34'73   78–8636
ISBN 0–664–32633–1

Photograph Acknowledgments

Here are the people and companies that so generously shared their world's fair photographs: Mr. Michael Pender, World's Fair Collectors Society, Inc.; Mrs. Sherman F. Gilpin; Miss Mildred E. Hardman; Miss Marty Von Rosenstiel; American Express Company; The Free Library of Philadelphia; The Smithsonian Institution; Pan American World Airways, Inc.; General Electric Company; Eastman Kodak Company; Westinghouse Electric Corporation; United Airlines; RCA Photo Library; United States Steel Corporation; Borden, Inc.; General Electric Lighting Institute; Old York Road Historical Society; United States Department of the Interior, National Park Service; Johns-Manville Corporation; and Association of American Railroads.

Contents

A fair is the hiss of a Roman candle,
a soft explosion,
and brilliants blazing
in the night.
And, like a candle, a fair is inevitably snuffed out.

Official Souvenir Book of the New York World's Fair 1964–1965. By the Editors of Time-Life Books

A Fair for All Reasons

American history is filled with fairs. Almost any reason was good enough to have a fair.

Elkanah Watson started fairs in the United States in 1810, and the only reason he had was sheep raising. He thought it was a good occupation and wanted to interest all his neighbors in sheep. The Berkshire Cattle Show set a pace that most American fairs have followed since 1810. Elkanah's suggestion that they have a parade, a prayer from a local minister, an anthem by a choir, and a speech by a famous citizen began a form that all fairs have followed.

Even Mrs. Watson should have her share of the credit. When Elkanah found that the local ladies were not attending the fair, he announced that his wife would be giving out the prizes. Since that day, women have always played an important role in American fairs.

No sooner had American fairs begun than they were almost stopped. On Wednesday, January 29, 1834, a group of merchants, storekeepers, and businessmen met in Philadelphia. They planned to put an end to fairs in the United States.

"It's immoral," insisted one man, "the way fairs take money out of the pockets of poor widows!"

"All sorts of evils and mischiefs arise from fancy fairs," claimed one indignant shopkeeper.

When pressed for details, he admitted that his business had fallen off 50 percent the previous Christmas season because his regular customers had spent all their money buying gifts at a fancy fair. Besides, the men argued, many widows had to support their children by selling "the products of the needle." Fancy fairs made a specialty of selling donated handsewn articles.

"It's evil when people who can afford to work for nothing compete with people who have to earn their living by making the same articles," a minister in the group argued.

There was a near-riot at this point when the meeting was broken up by a large group of citizens. But the merchants found another meeting place and published their ideas in a pamphlet that did nothing to stop America's interest in fairs.

America's reasons *for* fairs were far more important than any reasons for not having fairs.

As the United States began spreading westward and southward, communication became more difficult. Farmers in Kentucky wondered how farmers in other areas managed to plow hilly and rocky land. Some farmers discovered problems they would have to solve for themselves because no one had answers—for example, California farmers had to find a way to cope with gophers or a southern farmer needed a way to separate his wheat from the garlic that grew with it. Mechanics' Institutes were formed so that farmers, engineers, artists, manufacturers, and just plain tinkerers could share their ideas. Every year, in several large cities across the country, there was a Mechanics' Fair to show the best inventions and discoveries.

The first "here today—gone tomorrow cities" for fairs were built of tents during the Civil War. The U.S. Sanitary Commission was responsible for taking care of the sick and wounded Northern soldiers. But the Commission had no money or supplies by 1864. Someone thought of having a fair in each of several large cities, and the tents were set up in city squares or parks.

"Sanitary Fairs" used every means of parting the fairgoer from his money. Admission was only 50 cents, but after the visitor had entered the first tent, his money kept dwindling. In one aisle an elegant silver sword and a handsome saddle were exhibited—to be sent to the "favorite" general who received the most votes at a dollar a vote. A tent filled with paintings cost another dollar. A young girl mailed a letter to her soldier boyfriend, paying thirty times the actual cost of a stamp when she mailed it from "the Sanitary." Every person in the city was asked to donate to the fair as well as to contribute articles to be sold. Not even children were immune—whole schools made knitted mittens or wax flowers.

When they were not busy buying, Sanitary Fair visitors looked at pitiful displays—a rebel uniform captured at Gettysburg, a loaf of bread from Libby Prison, and an American flag made of scraps by a prisoner in Andersonville. Patriotic Northerners made a point of wearing their paper collars and cuffs—because the South represented cotton. At the end of a week or two, "the Sanitaries" closed with an auction that managed to get money for even the most unattractive items that had not been sold. Then the tents were folded up and carried away to another large city for the next fair.

No matter what the reason was for having fairs, Americans loved them all. There was magic in the temporary cities and buildings that would be there today, but completely gone away by tomorrow. It was not just the rich people who went to fairs—or even the poor. The people who went were the ones who had the ability to see that something unusual was about to happen, and then had the good sense to interrupt their humdrum lives to go see what was happening.

The old fair cities are gone now—like an optical illusion—leaving behind only a few reminders that they really were there once. What were those mysterious cities like? Who were the people who walked on streets now overgrown with grass and who had an early glimpse of the wonders that would soon come and change their lives?

Here is your ticket . . . The admission gate is just ahead.

1

New York's "Palace of Crystal" 1853

Seventy-seven years had passed since the signing of the Declaration of Independence. Business was good, and the steam engine (between frequent explosions) was beginning to change life in the United States. But the American people were still far from independent.

They still shipped their raw wool to England to be turned into cloth to make coats and suits. They bought their fine glassware from Austria, their dishes and window glass from France and England, and their boots from American boot shops that employed foreign workmen and used French leather. Rich ladies said only Irish hands could make flax into proper lace, and no one could make silk roses for hats like the French. All their works of art and other beautiful objects came from Europe.

There was not a single public art museum in any city and only one national collection in the country, the Smithsonian Institution in Washington City. Most libraries were private and very particular about the people they allowed to read their books. In a city growing as fast as New York (by this time over 515,000 people!), there was a great need for a metropolitan museum for arts and science.

A group of New York businessmen were looking for some way to bring the products of human efforts in the world together and compare notes. Some new inventions might be born—or at least some germs of thought planted. Two years before, some of the men had been to a great fair in London, England. America had never had a real fair. And certainly most Americans had never seen an elegant building like the Crystal Palace in London. The businessmen thought it might be possible to build such a fairyland of glass and iron in New York City. They would call it the Exhibition of the Industry of All Nations.

In a remote section of the city (where 42d Street crossed Fifth Avenue) the group leased an odd-shaped plot of ground for one dollar for five years. It was not the best piece of land on the outskirts of the city and it backed up against the Croton Reservoir. Folks suggested that would be handy in case there was a fire. And the Sixth Avenue and Fourth Avenue horse railways could be extended to carry people out to the fairgrounds.

All spring, New Yorkers collected on the terrace of the Croton Distributing Reservoir to watch the building of America's first "palace." Hordes of adults and children wandered in and out of the building, while the workmen struggled to follow the architects' plans. The men were not used to handling iron except for the building of large ugly warehouses. And they had never coped with joining iron and glass or used such large panes of glass before. The builder of the London Crystal Palace had tried to design the American Crystal Palace to exactly the same plan, but it simply would not fit on the odd-shaped lot. So two other architects, Carstensen and Guildermeister, tried to adapt the plans to fit. They had problems on top of problems.

The building was not just a simple rectangle. The first floor was in the shape of an octagon, and the second floor was shaped like a Greek cross. Over the top of it all, there was a huge dome. Soon workers discovered that on hot days the "interior vapors" leaked down on them from the dome, and on a rainy day everything leaked. The work might have been much easier if only the crowds of busybodies coming out from the city every day and wandering underfoot could be eliminated. Only during the final week were the doors closed to them so the work might be finished.

The business part of the city was around the Battery, at the south end of Manhattan Island. But now the city was slowly moving northward. The fashionable families were moving uptown, and their elegant mansions on Greenwich Street, where the edge of town used to be, were now inhabited by immigrants.

Only a few spring events had taken people's minds away from the building of the palace. One was the terrible train wreck on May 6. A train, speeding along at 50 miles an hour, plunged through a drawbridge that had been raised to let a steamboat pass. The engine, baggage car, smoking car, and three passenger coaches all sank in the river, drowning most of the passengers. Many of the dead were doctors, returning home from a medical convention in the city. The engineer and fireman escaped, and were promptly arrested and charged with manslaughter.

That same week the annual parade of schoolchildren took place. Most impressive were the poor boys of one orphan school—all dressed alike and marching barefoot. The newspaper next morning called them

> Bright-eyed little Yankees, in the face of every one of whom was the intention to look out for number one . . . fearless, careless, obstreperous little fellows. The same little individu-

The nation's first world's fair was in a Crystal Palace built of glass and iron

als who, after a few more presidents have been sworn into office, will own the railroads and be the victims of each other's recklessness in plunging over drawbridges and in running opposing engines into each other.

Many people wondered why New York needed a Crystal Palace fair to show them cultural things when what really was needed was a way to prevent railroad accidents and steam boiler explosions. Meanwhile, there were grim mutterings about whether the fair would ever open. Displays from other countries did not come when promised. Even the displays from various sections of America were slow in arriving. The building was nowhere near finished when the first "opening day" came and went.

Out-of-towners, called "provincials" by New Yorkers, arrived for the fair and were directed to other places in the city. Barnum's Museum drew huge crowds to see its trained fleas. Robert Heller performed magic stunts at the Chinese Hall. In Castle Garden, Louis Jullien's orchestra of 100 men featured a 10-year-old girl singer named Adelina Patti. The Hippodrome had a theater-in-the-round with ancient Greek and Roman festivals. There, the audience had more than they bargained for one night when the dress of a young actress caught fire from a candle footlight that had no globe over it. Frankenstein's "Panorama of Niagara" was billed as "not just a series of pretty pictures but a series of visibly realized natural effects." Or the travelers might prefer Jones's Pantoscope, where they saw a panorama of daguerreotype pictures of the overland journey to California. But the outstanding shows of the year were two versions of the same book—Harriet Beecher Stowe's *Uncle Tom's Cabin*. The Aikens version of the play was at the National Theater, while the Conway version at the Barnum Theater boasted wonderfully emotional scenes plus a happy ending.

The Fourth of July (another possible opening day when there was no opening) was celebrated loudly as usual. Newspapers warned that every pack of firecrackers averaged one burned hand, an eye put out, or a riot begun when the noise startled horses into bolting away. Other serious fires might have been avoided if grocery store owners had learned not to display fireworks for sale in windows where the sun shone in and ignited the gunpowder.

"It was gunpowder out of which our liberty sprang," people said. "With fireworks, our children will find out very naturally that it is a fight being celebrated, and the fires of freedom will keep warm in their breasts."

By July, it was so hot that everyone who could afford to get out of the steamy city had already left. The editor of *Knickerbocker Magazine* wrote that someday he intended to tell his readers about the Crystal Palace, but right now he was at his summer home along the Hudson River. There he was living down in the cellar, eating tomatoes and rice, and taking icy sponge baths all day long to keep cool.

Large active groups were trying to convince the city managers that they should make a park out of the woods in the central part of the island—they might even call it "Central Park." "Parks are the lungs of the city," they argued.

The Crystal Palace was really going to be an "upper-class fair" —planned and paid for by prominent men of the city who hoped to show that mere wealth, without the refinements of wealth, would only corrupt morals and degrade character. What surprised those fair planners was that thousands of the working classes were heartily enjoying the idea of a fair and making their own plans to attend it.

The average mechanic earned about $600 a year. His family paid about $8.50 a month to live in four rooms on a third floor in the city. The family grew fat on ham and hominy. Beef cost 12½ cents a pound, but a careful housewife could buy bone and gristle for 8 cents and make soup. Such items as chicken and fresh fruits (except for apples—a shilling for half a peck) were out of the question. For fuel, the mechanic paid $18 a year for 3 tons of coal, a load of pinewood, and a few barrels of charcoal to use for the ironing. His family's lights cost about $10, since candles cost 16 pence a pound and burning fluid was up to 22 cents a quart. He paid $5 a year to join a library because he could not afford to buy books, $12 a year for railroad tickets to visit his parents in the country, and about $10 for a doctor and all the medicines his family needed. Another $10 bought his family two thirds of one of the back pews in church, and $5 went for taxes. By the time clothing and household needs were taken care of, the mechanic's family would have to scratch the bottom of the penny bank to pay 50 cents each to go to the Crystal Palace. But they did find the money.

The biggest shock to the fair planners was the ramshackle village built of plaster and bits of wood that grew up around the Palace even before it was completed. One day there was a grog-gery where the thirsty workmen could eat their dinners. The next day there were two. Soon dozens of shacks had been slapped up haphazardly by owners each wanting to do his own thing.

Two weeks before Opening Day, a violent thunderstorm hit the Crystal Palace, splattering the worst hailstones seen in years onto the glass walls and dome, which was still unfinished. Several of the shanties outside collapsed on top of their customers, but no one was hurt. Posters of large beasts advertising the shanty sideshows were torn to tatters. The merry-go-round began turning in the wind, flinging its bucket seats high into the air. Someone thought to load heavy barrels into the seats to hold them down. Then the wind picked up speed, and the barrels were hurled as if from a giant slingshot into the shanties nearby, knocking down walls as though they were playing cards. Huge quantities of rainwater poured through the unfinished Palace dome. But the Palace weathered the hurricane—to the surprise of many people.

In no time at all, the shanty village rose again. By the week before the July 14 opening, visitors had to weave their way past all sorts of "amusements." One shack had wax figures whose faces drooped so badly in the summer heat that the personages of wax aged considerably between 10 A.M. and 4 P.M. A summer tavern served "refections"—just light meals for the not-so-hungry. There was no food inside the Palace until September, and then it was too expensive for most fairgoers.

An ice-cream trader had a booth next to a hardware vendor who sold "cooling drinks" and seemed always to be polishing his glass goblets. He could not say his drinks were soda water, because only an apothecary could legally sell soda water. Other booths offered a bearded French lady with a full mustache, a three-legged rooster and a five-legged calf, dancing bears, rattlesnakes "of loving and tender disposition," dwarfs, giants, a mummified pig, an alligator, and a mermaid with "a living tail." One man advertised "cupping, bleeding, and toothdrawing" in his booth.

People with space to rent opened "boarding houses" and plas-tered advertisements all over the tombstones of a nearby ceme-tery. A department store advertised "Crystal Palace carpets" for sale. Then there was "Crystal Palace ice cream," "Crystal Stables" with rent-a-horses, "The Crystal Hall of Pleasure" (quickly closed down by the police), and even a "Crystal Fruit Stall" which sold oranges and bananas in every state of decomposition.

All night before the opening, frantic last-minute jobs were done. Workmen tested the galleries for strength. They uncovered and dusted the statues, nailed down a red carpet on the speaker's platform, and unpacked the last of the wooden crates. Only half the exhibits had arrived, but there were enough to keep people busy for their first visit. Artists were still putting the final touches to painting the dome. Outside, the heaps of garbage were cleaned off all the city's streets, and sidewalk vendors were fined $5 for not keeping their carts out of the way. The Palace was as ready as it ever would be.

The crowds began collecting early on July 14 to watch the excitement. But only those who had paid $10 for a season ticket were allowed in that first day. Ten dollars was two weeks' wages for some and ten weeks' wages for a child lucky enough to work in a shoe factory.

The exhibitors arrived before 8 A.M. All morning, stagecoaches with drums, bugles, and boxes strapped to the roof stopped and emptied their contents of men, women, children, musicians, soldiers in colorful uniforms, and people who came to open their shanties for the early-morning business. The crowd would have been even larger, but many people had gone into the city to follow the President and the procession up the avenue to the Palace.

The day was hot and humid. Railway companies had ordered their drivers to allow the horses to go no faster than a smart pace for fear of having the streets littered with horse carcasses as they had been a few weeks earlier. Little boys sold fans for 3 cents each and the crowd kept the fountain keepers at the city water fountains busy selling 3-cent glasses of water. By 1:00 P.M. they were getting impatient. They had no idea that it was pouring rain a few miles to the south, forcing the parade to scurry under cover until it let up.

Meanwhile, the shanty village was losing no money. On this day, most of the owners had hired spielers and hawkers to pull visitors into the area and coax them to part with their money.

"If you do not trust me, see what it says about my Ox in the *Daily Express,*" shouted one man about his Giant Ox.

The owner of a cockfight arena let his sign do the shouting for him:

THE PRESIDENT AND HIS SUITE
HAVE BEEN INVITED
AND
probably
WILL ATTEND THE PERFORMANCE

The spectators were all in a good humor. No one minded the frauds, such as the tiny printing on the signs or the mermaid with "the living tail." The unwritten rule seemed to be: If you can't afford to be cheated, don't spend your money.

Suddenly the waiting people saw handkerchiefs waving out of upstairs windows far down the avenue. The procession was coming. The Crystal Palace police, dressed in linen coats "fresh from the washtub," fanned out to make a circle around the doorway. The city police (they were wearing badges) formed a second ring, good-naturedly shoving back the people who were packed tight around the Palace doors.

Those on the edge of the crowd could see the helmets of the First Troop of Washington Greys gleaming in the sun, and soon President Franklin Pierce, with his hat off, could be spotted as he bowed to the waving hankies. Pierce had just been inaugurated and was very popular. People sympathized with him because he had an ailing wife and had just lost a young son in a railroad accident the previous winter. Shortly after the President entered the Palace, a carriage and six arrived with Secretary of War Jefferson Davis. There seemed to be a surplus of military uniforms entering what some people had called "the palace of peace." The band played "Hail Columbia" and "Yankee Doodle," while the governors of several states, General Winfield Scott, Commodore James Stewart, and other important guests entered the beautiful wide doorways. The only other guests were the 600 season ticket holders.

The crowd outside the Palace seemed to have as much fun as the crowd inside. Every so often a cheer was heard through the windows or sounds of the choir singing Handel's "Hallelujah Chorus." In spite of the muggy weather, people were dancing outdoors. Inside, no one but Horace Greeley, editor of the *New York Tribune*, seemed to notice that the architects who had worked so hard had not even been invited to sit with the "important" people. There was not one representative of the workmen who had struggled to put it all together. Even the exhibitors had been told to stay in their sections rather than watch the opening events. The next day, July 15, the Crystal Palace would be open to anyone who could pay the 50 cents to go inside. The crowd seemed perfectly content to wait.

Most of the folk who streamed into the Palace all summer were from the country, where the "provincial" press had written about the exhibition in more glowing terms than New York City papers. Old folks, who knew they would never see another such fair in their lives, had saved their pennies to see the "Cristial Palace." The halls were filled with them trying to find a place to sit down. There were no seats that were not part of an exhibit. People could not lean on the banisters, because the varnish stayed sticky all summer. There was no place to eat inside, and no comfort stations until after September.

Out-of-town travelers were thrilled with their first view of New York City. The newspapers had told them how it would be. First they could see the clouds—that was the dust that always hung over the big city. Then they would see perpendicular lines that looked like a leafless forest. Those were the masts of ships in the harbor —the first sight of the city. Although the Crystal Palace was big, it was not tall. Rising tallest on the skyline were the spires of Trinity Church.

All spring, ladies everywhere had been buying up gray material to make traveling dresses. Gray did not show the dirt and dust from railroad and stagecoach travel.

Most men wore plain brown linen "wrappers" to protect their clothes from travel dust, and patent leather shoes which did not have to be blacked every day. An umbrella covered with a neat oilcloth sheet was used as both a cane and a cover if it stormed. Men usually traveled light, carrying only a carpetbag. But a man traveling with his wife needed at least a trunk and a bandbox.

Visitors to the city were warned to beware of the hackney coach drivers, who had just upped their prices 50 percent because of "heightened expenses of rent and increased competition." While Londoners rode in hackneys to their Crystal Palace for 25 cents, New Yorkers had to pay from $1.50 up, depending on how easily they could be tricked into paying more. The omnibus and cars (pulled by horses) took people to the fair for only a dime or sixpence a mile.

Five kinds of hotels were available. For about $2.50 a day, one

person could stay at the Howard or the Astor and enjoy an elegant
drawing room, a reading room, and bounteous food. The Claren-
don, Carlton, or Union Place attracted quiet gentlemen and their
families. Uptown there were monster hotels with huge mirrors
where one paid $3 a day, but where managers could charge up to
$100 a week for a family. Hotels like the Western, National, Clin-
ton, United States, and Fulton cost $2 a day. Cheapest of all were
the houses, where a bachelor could have a small room with a bed
and light for 25 cents to $1 a night and meals for 50 cents a day.

Since so many of the people coming to the exhibition had never
been in New York City (or in any other large city), the *New York
Times* warned country people how it would be on their first night:

> Will we ever be able to sleep with such a racket in the streets?
> Doesn't the city ever go to bed? The street seems as full as if
> everybody is hurrying to and from the Crystal Palace. . . . Was
> that a call for us? Somebody hailed the house. . . . Hark, a
> wagon stopt at the door. They are entering the next house.
> Let's go to sleep. It is almost midnight. Was that a cry of fire?
> Is it our house? There must have been a town meeting near
> here. . . . Did we top our candle? and let off the gas? What is
> it that fills the room with light then? Oh, it's from the lamp-
> post.

Choosing a place to eat in the city posed more problems. Where
there was a great deal of plate glass, visitors could expect to pay
large prices. A restaurant with dirty tablecloths or many people
around the bar would have low prices, but low quality food as well.
The prices on the menu were not to be relied on either, because
many restaurants charged more at night than the menu prices.
Strangers were warned not to drink any more of the Croton water
than necessary, because it was full of vermin, and to beware of
food sold on the streets.

Seven thousand people poured through the three massive entrances of the Crystal Palace on July 15. Confusion resulted because the tickets came in three different colors. The blue-ticket
holder could not be admitted through the pink-ticket door. But

Inside, the palace looked like fairyland to the visitors

the good humor of the crowd was still evident as they trudged around the huge palace to enter through the proper door.

Inside was fairyland! As far as eye could see, there was glass supported by long rows of graceful iron arches. The iron had been painted a rich cream color with touches of red, yellow, and blue tints. The ceiling was painted in octagons of blue, white, red, and cream. In the center, the awestruck visitor could look a hundred feet straight up to the dome. The rays of the sun streamed through its latticed ribs, touching its painted arabesques of white, gold, and blue. Silver stars shimmered around the openings in the dome.

The best way to get an overall view of the exhibits was to climb one of the twelve staircases and walk around the gallery, looking down on the crowd. From the center was a good view of Baron Marochetti's much-talked-about statue of George Washington on horseback and the equally disliked Carew statue of Daniel Webster. Horace Greeley complained that Washington looked like a bag of meal thrown over the horse's back. His face was Franklin's and his body was short and squat, his legs were too long and his head didn't match up with any other parts. The right hand, holding his hat, looked as if it was twisted with palsy. And to make it worse, the horse was lifting its forefoot as if to paw the earth violently, while its hind leg was raised as if going on a gentle trot. Still, Greeley concluded, the statue of Washington was a work of art compared to the disgraceful statue of Daniel Webster.

"The wood-carver who makes figureheads for ships would lose his customers if he supplied such a work of art as this!"

Only a third of the exhibits were American. But seeing the best products of Europe firsthand, many Americans realized they no longer had to be afraid of competition. This country had all the raw materials needed to turn out beautiful glassware, woodwork, and china. It also had many artisans who could do the work. All the country needed was encouragement—and this it got at the Crystal Palace.

Even in London people had said Americans made the best da-

Fairgoers in 1853 could not wait until the exhibition was ready to open before they crowded the displays

guerreotypes. Some thought it was because the country had less fog and bluer skies. But actually it was because America had Mathew Brady, who could take excellent photographs under the worst of circumstances. People said he could even make ordinary people look as important as "literary giants." One photo collection of Indian warriors at the palace was being sent to London to have busts made of each Indian.

Americans were ahead of other countries in making firearms, too. Their rifles had been notorious for nearly a hundred years. The Colt revolver beat any gun sent from England, France, or Russia. One revolving rifle shot 60 times in succession in two and a half minutes. Americans spent so much more time in the saddle than Europeans that it was not surprising to find that American saddles were the best as well as the most comfortable. Although most saddles were made of buckskin, the best were of hogskin. A lady's sidesaddle, with a long skirt to keep her dress clean, could be bought at the fair for $15.

Americans were at their very best, however, when it came to inventing machines to make work easier. The McCormick reaper was already well known. It sold for $115 or, with the mowing attachment, $140. One farmer's "labor-saving machine" at the Palace threshed, cleaned, and put 100 bushels of wheat a day into bags, using two horses as power. For southern farmers, there was a machine to separate garlic from wheat. Some plows were for steep hillsides, and the ditchdigger (a dozen shovels arranged around a wheel) could be pulled by a span of horses and one man.

Among the inventions for ladies was a patent corn broom handle. It had a steel spring covered with teeth to snap down and bite into the broom, making a new corn broom in minutes. In fact, said the demonstrator, the farmer's wife could make the broom herself, "which is a vast step toward her independence."

Another invention to lighten a woman's workday was a washing machine tub with grooves on the inside bottom. When the handle was turned (no easy matter once clothes and water were inside), the clothes "washed themselves."

People complained because so many machines were displayed without a sign or a demonstrator to tell people what they were supposed to do. A large crowd collected around an item one day.

"It's some sort of fishnet," said one.

"Maybe it's to strain maple sap," another guessed.

One curious man finally tracked down the owner of the exhibit and discovered that he had been looking at a pair of snowshoes.

Everyone ignored the "Hands Off" signs, so most of the displays were behind glass. But this did not keep curious people from gaping long hours at the contents. Ladies hung over cases of artificial flowers and leaves dreaming of next spring's hat trimmings. Men packed around a case of oxhides from Tannersville, Pennsylvania. Oxhides that used to take four or five years to tan in a yard now took only days, using chemicals. Men strained for a look at hats made of silk, rabbit fur, wool, beaver, and nutria, and especially at a top hat that was collapsible.

"Don't I wish I could get through to them just!" a small boy was heard to mutter at the candy counter. Behind the glass case were spun-sugar butterflies, birds, and fruits; flowers in colored sugar; French chocolate rats and deer; and scenes of people spun out of sugar. American candymakers did not use dangerous ingredients for coloring or flavoring as European candymakers did. Poor children were in no danger, however. For them, the only sweets were "peanut cakes and 'lasses candy," made from the drainings of molasses off the floors and walls of the sugar refineries.

The humming whir of a huge wheel, with beams moving up and down or cogwheels to watch, stirred the public's enthusiasm. The large machines were polished and painted and decorated with flowers and gold flourishes. They were given names—like the "Henry Clay," which was a rocking beam engine of 60 horsepower made by Corliss and Nightingale. Or the "Southern Belle" made of iron mined in Alabama. Or the huge "Lawrence," which had the incredible power of 75 horses. Every detail of how an engine worked intrigued the fair visitor.

The "corn doctor" was very busy in 1853. A sewing machine had not been devised that could sew the upper part of a shoe onto the sole. The newest Paris shoes had the tops screwed onto the soles with brass screws. They did not shrink when the shoes got wet or expand the way the wooden pegs did in American-made shoes. But they were too expensive for most people. So fairgoers stood with aching feet and pounding corns, watching the newest shoe-making machine. Most men wore thick calfskin boots ($2). Women wore Lola Montez boots (65 cents to $1) and children had brogans (60 cents), while wealthier men could buy a pair of patent leather boots for $10 (more if the boots had ornamental stitching).

The star of the show was the electromagnetic telegraph invented by Samuel F. B. Morse. Only nine years before, the Government had set up the first trial line between Washington and Baltimore so Morse could prove that his telegraph really worked. Since then, 15,000 miles of telegraph lines had connected large cities on the East Coast. City newspapers now had a column headed "Telegraphic News." That meant it was the latest possible news—the editor filled the column at the last minute before the paper was printed, taking the news from the telegraph. Steamships leaving Europe now received telegraphic messages of the latest news and relayed it to the newspaper as soon as they arrived in port. That news was in a column marked "By Steamship" and it was only 10 to 14 days old!

The telegraph was called "one of those immortal discoveries that give character to an age." In other fairs to come, each one would have its special star of the show.

Some other inventions seen at the Palace were to make changes for people in the years ahead. Elisha Otis had invented an elevator —and next year he would install one in the Palace. His invention meant that someday buildings could be taller than four stories (after the discovery of constructing tall buildings with a steel skeleton). Whitworth was displaying a measuring machine that could measure a millionth part of an inch—not a very dramatic kind of invention, but one that had to be made before other machines could be invented. Until then, an engineer could never get a part made for his machine that was precisely the right size. No two shops—not even two workmen—could make an exact copy of any machine part until Whitworth's invention.

The electrotype that people were looking at in the Palace could make many copies of pictures from engraved copperplates. Now it would be possible for every child to have schoolbooks with some pictures inside. Books themselves would be much cheaper, so even the poor could hope to have at least a Bible of their own.

One reason why so much business came from Europe into the northeastern states was that ship captains knew where they were going. Very good charts had been made of the rocky northeastern coastline even before the Revolution. But for the middle and southern states charts were useless because of the constantly shifting sandy bottoms of the harbors. At the Palace, the U.S. Coast Survey showed fairgoers how they were charting thousands of miles of the coastline. Steamships like the *Arctic* and the *Arabia,* which had just broken all records by crossing the Atlantic in less than ten days, would soon be able to use other ports as well as New York.

Interior decorating was a new idea in 1853. Even wealthy people who had seen elegance in Europe were happy with plain, whitewashed walls at home in America. At the Palace, for the first time many women discovered there were other ways to make a house look like a home. One of these was by painting with wax and color—called "encaustic." The people of Pompeii had used the technique, and so it was known that the color would last over fifteen hundred years! The colors did not darken, as they did in oil paintings, and could be polished just by rubbing. Another decorative art, almost unknown in the United States, was fresco painting, done on the wet plaster of ceilings and walls. It was very hard to do, because the artist could not erase his mistakes.

At 10:00 P.M. every bell in the Palace rang, and the people walked slowly toward the doors. The cleaners came in then to do their work. But looking back, the visitors could see the dome and glass walls lighted by gas and found it so charming that soon there had to be a "Gas Light Opening."

On Friday, September 2, a huge crowd was inside to see the Crystal Palace lighted for the first time. Four thousand burners flamed—only 30 less than were used for all the streetlights in the entire city! The light coming from within gave the building an "aerial lightness" people had not seen before, and it looked larger than ever. All the machines were working with thumps, squeaks, and whirs. A small orchestra struggled valiantly to be heard above the din. Every six seconds a bright light flashed fleetingly through the glass at one side—the new revolving light designed for the Cape Hatteras lighthouse.

In the middle of September, all the schoolchildren of New York City were given a day at the Palace. Each one clutched 5 cents, which was to be given to the Washington Monument collection. The cornerstone for the monument in Washington City had been laid a few years back, but donations were very hard to get. Every day a few more dollars were collected for the fund from the fairgoers.

Except for their donations, these New York children may not have been too different from the little boy who had gone with his school to the Crystal Palace in London just two years before. He had written in his diary:

> We were told not to forget this and to make a note of that. What do I remember out of it all? The Koh-i-noor diamond because it was so small a thing to have such a fuss made about it, the statue of the Greek slave because one of the boys afterwards said that had it not been for a promise that tea and cakes would begin immediately, he would have hit that Greek slave over her unprotected head in order to begin a row, and a group of stuffed monkeys playing a game of quoits.

The statue of the Greek Slave was made by a young American, Hiram Powers, who had gone to Italy to study art. No one had ever noticed him until his statue had caused a sensation at the London Crystal Palace. When it finally arrived at the New York Crystal Palace, people also admired it. But the art critics put it with the Greek and Roman exhibits since it was done in that style of art. There were hardly any works of American artists at the palace. This would be the last American fair ever to make that mistake.

The Exhibition of the Industry of All Nations in New York did not actually have a closing day. It just faded away. The original businessmen who had put up the money to pay for the fair had sold off their shares of stock. It was the second and third shareholders who got stuck with paying the bills. The idea that the Crystal Palace might become a permanent metropolitan museum of art and science that the city needed never did take hold, not even when the directors invited the genius of all showmen, P. T. Barnum, to become the president.

On October 5, 1858, the building was almost empty. The money was gone. A fire started in the night and swept through the Palace. Although it was built of iron and glass, its floors and roof were wood. The Crystal Palace was finished.

But it was obvious that America was not finished with fairs. A book published in 1854 already had some ideas for the next event. One idea was to have concessions so that people might have a choice of places to eat within the fair. By the time the restaurant opened inside the Crystal Palace, the food was so expensive that only the wealthiest patrons could satisfy their appetites there. In addition, there was no way for fair visitors to leave the Palace and come in again without buying another ticket. Other suggestions for the next fair were chairs on wheels, seats for tired visitors, and the right to publish an official catalog. The book also said there was no need to make each fair bigger—it was more important that fairs be held in rotation in different state capitals so everyone would have a chance to see a fair.

The best result of the Crystal Palace exhibition was that Americans never again felt their own work was inferior. In another twenty years, they would be planning their nation's 100th birthday party with a huge fair to show off the wonders they were able to produce.

In their own strange ways, many parts of the Crystal Palace fair survived to appear once more at the next fair. One of these was the shantytown with all its oddest inhabitants—alligators, quick foods, midgets and giants, five-legged pigs, snakes, and frauds. Snapped corn surfaced at the next fair as "popped corn." The telegraph kept reappearing until, in years ahead, it gave way to the wireless telegraph, the telephone, and then television.

Best of all, New Yorkers set to work establishing their own museum of science and art—The Metropolitan. In the year following, one city after another realized the importance of having its own museums, libraries, and historical societies, where people could go without paying to see the arts and industries of all nations. Even though the Crystal Palace was not a city, the idea of city planning began with the Palace and with the clamor for a "Central Park." From this fair on, there was always a close tie between city planning and the "model city" that was the fairgrounds.

Before there was another chance for a large fair, fighting between the states broke out and threatened to put an end to the United States before they were one hundred years old. By 1864, the South was in bad shape and the North was in financial trouble, too. During the war, the U.S. Sanitary Commission was responsible for taking care of the sick and wounded Northern soldiers. When the Commission ran out of supplies and money, someone suggested that a big fair be held in each of several large cities.

The Sanitary Fairs were held in tents—actually they were the first "here today—gone tomorrow cities." Northerners, wearing paper collars and cuffs (because cotton ones represented the South), paid 50 cents to go inside the tents, but their purses were kept busy from the moment they went in. Not even a drink of water was free. Young girls gladly paid thirty times the actual cost of a stamp just to mail letters to their boyfriends from "the Sanitary." Fairgoers voted for their "favorite" generals for a dollar a vote. The prizes, awarded to the winning generals, were elegant silver dress swords and handsome saddles. Every person in the city was asked to give a day's wages to the fair as well as to donate articles that could be sold for the highest possible prices. Children at school knitted mittens and made wax flowers to sell. The toy counters at the fair featured lady dolls with handmade wardrobes of hoopskirted dresses, stuffed animals, and toy drums. Overhead was a large sign to remind the buyers of their duty: "Every child that buys a toy heals the wound of some brave boy."

When the war ended at last, the Southern states were desperately poor and in no mood to join the Northerners, who wanted to celebrate the nation's 100th birthday with a fair larger than any the country had ever seen.

2

Philadelphia's "Centennial City" 1876

Young people in 1876 had to make most of their own entertainment at home. But even taffy pulls, picnics, home readings, and singing societies could grow boring after a while. When word leaked out that there might be a huge fair for the nation's 100th birthday, teen-agers who might be able to get to Philadelphia to see it could hardly wait to hear more about it.

Only twenty-three years had passed since Americans had held their first real fair in a Crystal Palace. They had been unsure of themselves and their homemade products then, but now America was one hundred years old. No nation in the world had ever seen such a deluge of inventions and discoveries as had appeared in the United States just within the previous ten years!

An express train that sped across the country (sometimes at fifty miles an hour!) in only three and a half days . . . a telegraph that sent two messages at the same time over a single wire . . . a machine that could send voices over wires—these were the promised marvels that made people pack their valises and head for the "Centennial City."

Celebrating the Centennial was not a very popular idea at first. The depression in 1873 had caused many businessmen to panic, and salaries were still going down. A farmer's helper earned 60 cents a day, instead of the 75 cents he had earned a year before. There was little money for patriotic causes. The Washington Monument committee was still trying to collect donations to build an obelisk in Washington, D.C. Congress finally voted some money to finish the pile of granite blocks that was still only 174 feet high. Another committee in Philadelphia was working feverishly to restore the old State House to the way it had looked a hundred years

On Opening Day, Centennial crowds covered the
roof, the courtyard, and even the statues to hear the
choir of a thousand voices

before when the Declaration of Independence was signed there.

"Don't have a fair in Philadelphia!" some people argued. "That Quaker city is against everything new."

But Philadelphia had a park and an open field with space enough for the kind of fair its directors had in mind. They were not thinking of one large building—but perhaps a hundred buildings! A dignified name was chosen—"The International Exhibition of Arts, Manufactures, and Products of the Soil and Mine." But the title had no ring to it. People simply called it "The Centennial" from the start.

As soon as work on the fair began, the grounds around the fair started sprouting shanties. Before the fair opened, they were advertising their tempting offerings. There would be alligators, a 602-pound fat lady, a bearded woman, a five-legged cow and a two-legged horse, an educated pig, "wild men" from Borneo, girls who danced the Can Can (except when arrested by the police), the gymnastic feats of M. Léotard who wore a shockingly tight suit, and plenty of food to eat. Even before opening day, people walking past the "Honky-tonk Midway" smelled the goodies to be bought there—hot roasted potatoes, ice cream, oysters from the Delaware River, peanuts (not allowed inside the fair because the broom brigade objected to sweeping up the shells), cakes, pies, bologna sausage, polished apples, caramels, oranges, and lemonade.

All winter, Philadelphians took their visitors through Centennial City while work wagons tore over the rutted mud paths, trains chugged up to buildings to be unloaded, and workmen struggled to put together structures that would be torn down again within the year. For a while it appeared the fair might never be finished, but Congress voted some money to help, since the fair might take people's minds off the depression and the government's political scandals. Curious sightseers had to step carefully around packing cases, straw packing material, boards, nail kegs, trash, and mud.

Finally gardeners patted hillsides of clay with their shovels and in a burst of optimism planted "Please do not step on the grass" signs everywhere.

Travel was not easy in 1876, but people could put up with any discomfort for a fair. Thousands poured into the depots and hailed hackney cabs or Centennial carriages (which looked like hearses) to carry them to the nearest hotel. Many very flimsy hotels had been set up for the fair. A better new one was the triangle-shaped Transcontinental. It was five stories high, but the guest who had to climb to the top floor was assured that the rooms up there so far above the dusty streets had "cleaner air and quieter nights." Rooms cost upward of $5 a day, including three meals and tea. The headwaiter assigned each guest to a table, but all children ate with their nurses at one large table.

The big day came on May 10. An early-morning rain washed the streets and laid the dust, but it didn't dampen spirits. Thousands of visitors rushed for the turnstiles, where they were supposed to pay for their entrance with a 50-cent note. But by now there was a shortage of 50-cent notes. People waved their quarters and dollar bills at the turnstile keepers and when they refused to take the money, the impatient fairgoers simply jumped over the stiles.

The rush was not to see President Grant. He had lost almost all the popularity he had enjoyed just after the Civil War, and everyone was glad to see him leaving the presidency. One of the most popular men in the United States was Dom Pedro II, the emperor of Brazil. He had become emperor as a boy of five and now, as a grown man, was visiting a country that he openly admired. With him standing beside Grant, there would be more applause and fewer hisses.

By 10 A.M., the orchestra had launched into a long musical program that included several patriotic tunes, since the United States still did not have a national anthem. Then they played the $5,000 tune. Richard Wagner, the most famous composer living, had been paid that amount to compose a Centennial March for the occasion. Everyone hated it and even Wagner said, "The best part about it was the money."

At the stroke of noon, just as a choir of a thousand voices finished Handel's "Hallelujah Chorus," there was a one-hundred-gun salute. Flags fluttered up the poles on every building and a procession of 4,000 notables marched through the Main Exhibition Hall

The ladies raised enough money to build their own Women's Building when told there would be no space for their exhibits at the Centennial

to the Machinery Hall. When half of them arrived (the other half got lost in the turmoil), President Grant and Dom Pedro turned a handle that sent the huge Corliss engine churning into action. Immediately all the other engines started, since they were run by the Corliss. The fair was on!·

Dom Pedro's wife, Empress Theresa, was to open the Women's Building with Mrs. Grant, but since the President's wife got lost in the crowd, the Empress pulled a silken cord to start the engine there. A great-granddaughter of Benjamin Franklin named Mrs. E. D. Gillespie had helped to raise millions of dollars for Centennial City through her committees of women all over the United States. Their reward was to be a special Women's Section in the Main Exhibition Hall. But when the fair directors told Mrs. Gillespie at the last minute there would be no money or space for the Women's Section, she was so furious that the ladies of her committees raised enough money in three months to have their own building. They topped it off with an engine of their own and a lady engineer to run it. Women hoped that now their abilities would be recognized beyond their use of the needle and thread. Across the street from the Women's Building, the cannons of the Government Building were pointed playfully straight at them.

American fairgoers never dreamed how huge a fair could be! It was a city of 249 buildings! There were 84 miles of asphalt paths to follow—and that did not count the miles of walking *inside* the buildings. Luckily, narrow-gage railroad engines with open cars carried footsore visitors around the grounds, stopping at each of the main buildings. The train ride cost only a nickel, but most people were nervous because it moved too fast—sometimes 8 miles an hour. People with more money could hire a rolling chair, pushed by a "chair boy," for an outrageous 60 cents an hour or $4.50 a day. People who walked looked on those riding in the chairs as lazy or else the victims of some strange illness. Only a very few men dared be seen in the chairs at all.

There was so much to see! Fairgoers were especially curious about the Orientals. Crowds had collected around the Chinese and Japanese workmen while they were working on their buildings and had commented loudly on everything from their clothing to the way they used a plane or a saw. Evidently the Far Easterners were curious about the odd Americans, too. The Japanese commissioner to the Centennial City wrote this report about fair visitors:

> The crowds come like sheep. Run here. Run there. Run everywhere. One man start, one thousand follow. Nobody can see anything. Nobody can do anything. All rush, push, tear, shout, make plenty noise, say "Damn" great many times, get very tired and go home.

Nobody went home from Centennial City saying it was beautiful. The fair was half over before the flowers, grass, or plants appeared. One person wrote, "The fountains were designed to convince the people there is no such thing as a pretty fountain." Most of the buildings looked like factories because they had large windows and skylights, just as factories had. The Main Exhibition Hall, largest in the world, was over a third of a mile long. Agricultural Hall was a gigantic barn, but the farm machinery inside was polished wood and gilded metal looking incapable of doing dirty farm jobs. Horticultural Hall, with a beautiful long garden in front,

Steam engines attracted crowds of admirers. This reproduction of one still performs at the Smithsonian Institution's "Centennial Exhibit"

was the closest to "1876-beautiful" with its glass windows and iron arches. Scattered among the factoryish buildings were many smaller ones that looked like little Victorian gingerbread cottages. In one area, several states had set up their own buildings, making Centennial City look like a model city.

The star of the fair was the huge Corliss engine. Men and women alike stood in awed silence, happily watching this super-machine's parts move in well-oiled symmetry. Just watching the engineer who tended the Corliss calmly reading his newspaper was exciting to the crowds. They cheered when he set down his paper, climbed a ladder with his oilcan, squirted the oil with his professional touch, climbed down, and picked up his newspaper once more. Folks talked respectfully about how the 700-ton Corliss had come to Philadelphia in 65 freight cars, and bet each other that its 1,500 horsepower could probably reach 2,500 horsepower.

The other engines, run by the Corliss, attracted just as much loving attention. People who lived miles from a farm watched the self-binding reaper do its work, and farmers watched fascinated while one machine jabbed 180,000 straight pins into pieces of paper and another turned out 40,000 bricks a day. The engines were painted in shiny enamel and trimmed with gold scrolls and flowers, each with a fancy emblem giving its name. One of the best-remembered sights of Centennial City was a full half mile of nothing but sewing machines, all sitting silent behind velvet ropes. Flocks of people hovered over a young lady who demonstrated the "Radiant Flat Iron." Inside the hollow iron was a gas flame made hotter by small drafts of air.

"But what makes the pressure of the gas and the drafts of air?" asked a bystander.

"I just shift my weight . . . as one always does when ironing," she answered sweetly and showed the audience she was standing on two bellows that pumped air and gas into the iron.

In future fairs, people would demand amusement areas with fun things to do. But the machines of 1876 were entertainment enough. Mark Twain had said the new typewriter invention "piles an awful stack of words on one page." For only 50 cents, a fairgoer could dictate a letter of his very own to a girl who typed it as he spoke. Nearby was an envelope-making machine that took flat papers, cut them, swished on glue, printed a stamp, folded, dried, and delivered a completed envelope in seconds. Everyone bought an envelope for his typewritten letter, but the most exciting part was licking the gum that stuck the envelope shut. That was a new idea.

Professor Moses G. Farmer astonished audiences with his generator and one-arc lamp. He claimed to have a lamp in every room of his home, but the one-arc lamp gave a very feeble light and people felt sorry for his wife who could have used a good kerosene lantern. There were more gaslight appliances on display than anyone had ever seen at one time before. One newspaper writer said, "Americans are the most gas-burning people in the world."

Thomas A. Edison showed admirers his telegraph system that sent two messages at the same time over a single wire. Edison was certainly a man to watch. He had just opened a research laboratory and told people he would turn out small inventions every few weeks and two important ones every year.

Professor Alexander Graham Bell, a well-known teacher of the deaf, seemed to be wasting his time on an invention that he claimed would let people talk to each other over a wire. But he managed to impress Emperor Dom Pedro II, who came to the fairgrounds on a Sunday when it was quiet enough to hear Bell's

Everyone wore hats in 1876, but the well-dressed boy or girl had a "Centennial Hat" with red, white, and blue ribbons

gadget (since the fair was not open). Dom Pedro listened and then shouted, "It talks!"

International Congresses on various subjects were planned in Philadelphia to coincide with the fair. Presiding over the Congress on Surgery was a British doctor named Joseph Lister. He told the doctors in his audience about his theory of germs and the absolute necessity for a surgeon to be extra clean. One famous doctor sitting in the audience was in the habit of stropping the knife on his shoe to sharpen it while he was operating on a patient. Another surgeon, the proud owner of a bushy set of whiskers, always held the operating instruments that he was not using in his mouth until he needed them. Neither of these doctors thought that Dr. Lister was referring to him when he accused surgeons of not being careful enough.

"The hottest summer in eighty years," said the newspapers, and soon these doctors had a small epidemic on their hands. "Centennial fever" came from drinking the water, sitting on the cool doorsteps at night, or from overeating, or from any one of a hundred suggestions. Doctors claimed the symptoms looked suspiciously like typhoid fever, but if that word leaked out, no one would come to the fair. The truth was that Centennial City was actually as large as a small city—but it did not have the drainage that a real city would have. The next fairs would have to be planned more carefully.

Even the fairgoers who did not get the fever were miserable as one sweltering day followed another. Other years, Philadelphians had closed their shutters in the summer, keeping the houses dark and cooler. They had put all their furniture in linen "bags" and replaced their hot carpets with grass rugs. But this year was different. Cousins and friends came to visit and to see the fair. Ladies discarded their fashionable "go to the Centennial" outfits, covered over their coolest dresses with a dust cloak, and just hoped nobody important would see them dressed so carelessly. The heat buckled the asphalt paths, and through their thin-soled shoes visitors felt as if they were walking over hot lava.

The only relief was at the cold drink concessions. Even for them, the fair directors had had to send north as far as Penobscot Bay to find cakes of ice. The Minnehaha Soda Fountain dispensed soda water in lemon, sarsaparilla, ginger ale, and birch beer flavors. A local druggist, Charles Hires, sold glasses of his famous herb tea that he called "root beer" for 3 cents each, while lemonade cost 10 cents. A new treat had been discovered two years before when Robert Green was trying to combine melted ice cream with soda water. His customers were hot and did not want to wait for the ice cream to melt, so he put them together. Now Centennial City was selling ice-cream sodas as fast as they could be made.

Americans were curious about each other in 1876. The fair had thrown together rich and poor, farmers and businessmen, backwoodsmen and professors, and people from many foreign nations. Crowds followed and pointed at people whose clothes were strange or who wore their hair differently. Yet the well-dressed American envied the Easterners in their saris and kimonos because they looked so cool. Curious fairgoers would even cluster around a bystander who stopped to buy something at a booth, often making suggestions or pointing out other things to buy. Everyone loved to hear the sound of customer and seller haggling over a price.

Many other sounds filled the air. Unfortunately, some of the musical sounds seemed to have been timed to go off all at the same moment. While two operatic singers were having a go at *Faust,* a pianist plunged into a Beethoven sonata, an organ pulled out all its stops, and one of the parade bands started up a march. Over top of all, the Centennial chimes in the tower of Machinery Hall often sounded. The official orchestra for the fair was under the direction of Jacques Offenbach. His concertmaster was a young man whose name would be found at many future fairs—John Philip Sousa.

Besides their ears, fair visitors were often led around by their noses. Some of the more pungent aromas were worse during the heat—like the sickening odor of the cement (a successful formula for making cement had not yet been found) and the "steamboat odor" coming from some of the restaurants. But from other areas wafted the smells of popcorn balls, buckwheat cakes, and a strange but pleasing odor that hung over the Oriental bazaars. Many people discovered incense and took some home with them. Outside the Vienna Bakery was the best smell of all—the baking of bread. American housewives made slightly sour, sawdusty, bread because they did not yet have good yeast.

Americans made unfortunate comparisons in the way their homes looked, too. At Centennial City, housewives saw pretty

"Kindergarten" was a brand-new idea, but many people thought it was dangerous to teach such young children. Fair visitors could observe the experiment

sample rooms with attractive wallpaper and furniture that looked comfortable. In the Turkish Restaurant, they found big soft ottomans they wanted at home, carpets and cool muslin curtains from India, dainty figurines from France, and pretty garden statues from Italy. They also saw a garish display by a New York store of furniture made entirely of mirrors and that, at least, they knew they didn't want.

American schools were about to change greatly, thanks to the fair. Teachers had been convinced that young people could not possibly handle tools, but the Russians showed up with an exhibit of schoolboy woodworking that would have put a professional to shame. Soon American schools would add industrial arts to the curriculum. For three years, educators had been hearing about "kinder-gartens" or, as some called them, "kitchen gardens." Now, at the fair, they could watch one in action. The little children, instead of turning into nervous wrecks as some doctors thought they might, seemed to love the new experience. Every school in the United States had been invited to send a picture to the Education Department at the fair, and across the country hundreds of photographs were taken.

When it came time to eat, Centennial City had many choices— planners remembered what the eating had been like at the Crystal Palace. Visitors could spend an outrageous $4.60 for a roast beef dinner at the Three Brothers of Provençal or settle for Viennese cake and a 25-cent cup of coffee at the Vienna Bakery. The Tunisian Café was recommended for patrons who liked exotic music with their meals. The Great Southern Restaurant, the Great American, and the Lunch Counter had reasonable prices. They were decorated in red, white, and blue, and above all, they served unlimited amounts of pickles.

Centennial City was expecting crowds over the Fourth of July —but no one could have foreseen what a multitude would descend on Philadelphia and the fair for that occasion. The celebration began on Saturday, July 1, took a slight rest on Sunday when nothing was open, then shifted into high gear for Monday and Tuesday.

The railroads took complete leave of system and sanity. Ticket agents refused to hand out train schedules because not one single train was running on schedule anyway. Trains passed platforms loaded with people. Valises were left everywhere except at the right stations, and hardly a single visitor arriving that weekend had any clothes to wear save those on his back. Restaurants ran out of food before Saturday night. Hotels were bulging—"important people" in the rooms and unimportant ones flopped on chairs in the lobbies. River steamboats were so loaded that their lower decks were almost in the water. Their captains refused to stop at landings where there were crowds waiting to get on, but they did consent to move within jumping distance of the wharf if a passenger wanted to get off. Hackney drivers demanded (and got) any price they wanted from customers. Horses reared and panicked in the streets at the sounds of fireworks and cap pistols (a wonderful new invention that year). Parades had to disperse because the watchers spilled over the sidewalks and clogged the streets.

In spite of it all, Centennial City visitors had a great time. Most of the ceremonies took place at Independence Hall, but along the

*Anyone who was brave enough could ride the slow-
moving Prismoidal Railway for a nickel*

streets glowed huge "illuminations," or displays brightly lighted with gas flares in many colors. Two hundred thousand people spent the Fourth of July in the fairgrounds, where it was cooler. They all dressed in their best, with red, white, and blue ribbons attached to hats, parasols, baby carriages, and suit lapels. Many colorful uniforms could be seen among the crowds as the marchers from different regiments took in the fair's sights. The Schuylkill River at the edge of the exhibition grounds was a crowded highway, with small steamboats, slender racing boats, and barges full to overflowing with passengers seated under striped awnings.

The river was the scene of several regattas and boat races during the fair. The New England whaleboat races were new to everyone who had not read *Moby Dick*. The crew wore blue nightcaps on their heads, wide sashes around their waists, and looked for all the world like pirates. Their boats were large and heavy. Each had a coxswain (who gave the orders and steered with a long oar), a harpooner, and five rowers (two sat on one side and three on the other). The crowd, entering into the spirit of the race, shouted from the shore, "Whale ahead!" and "Thar she blows!"

Close by the river was one of the marvels of modern transportation—the Prismoidal Railway for Rapid Transit. Visitors paid a nickel to ride over a ravine on the clumsy car straddling a wooden rail. They were sure the world would soon be traveling on monorails like this in every city. Almost a hundred years later, a monorail appeared at another world's fair, in Seattle, Washington, and people were still saying the same thing about it.

There were some Centennial City sights that young people told each other not to miss. One of these was the Sawyer Observatory. It was a round, glass-enclosed elevator that climbed a shaft 185 feet high for a real bird's-eye view of the fair. Another special sight was Commodore Oliver Perry's flagship *Lawrence*. The *Lawrence* had just been raised from the bottom of Erie Bay, where it had been sunk by the British sixty-three years before. When it sank, Perry had taken down his "Don't Give Up the Ship" flag, rowed over to another ship, and continued the fight. The third special sight was Old Abe, the bald eagle that had survived thirty battles of the Civil War with a Wisconsin regiment. A Southern general had said, "I would rather capture Old Abe than a whole brigade," because he knew what the eagle meant to the soldiers' morale. Not an amiable pet, the big bird bit admirers who came too close.

Centennial visitors were thrilled with the tropical gardens inside Horticultural Hall

There were a few sights that the Centennial could have done without—and many of them were never seen at later fairs. One was the Liberty Bell made entirely of plugs of tobacco. The Iowa State Building had two monstrous wreaths, looking very funereal —made of human hair. Venezuela had come up with an even worse exhibit—a picture of George Washington made from the hairs of Venezuela's revolutionary hero, Simón Bolívar. The Main Exhibition Hall was supposed to display everything made in America, but the cases full of corsets, cigars, and false teeth did not draw much of a crowd. There were, however, quite a few people looking over the tombstone display and admiring burial caskets that did not leak.

Besides the exotic plants and tall palm trees in Horticultural Hall, there were charming paths beside waterfalls and ponds. Everyone hoped this one building would last forever. Once an hour, the sounds of the orchestrion filled the huge hall. Although the music was played by an "electromagnetic orchestra" using rolls of paper with holes inscribed in it just like those used in a player piano, the sounds were very much like a real orchestra.

At the end of August, the Philadelphia newspapers barely mentioned the arrival of a statue made by a French sculptor named Bartholdi. But crowds collected to see it, because the pieces of the statue that had arrived were so gigantic. Pieces of a forearm, wrist, hand, fingers, parts of a torch, and what looked like a flame were laid on the ground beside a small lake. Fairgoers could hardly believe that this was only a small part of a very large statue that would someday be erected on an island in New York harbor.

Workmen put the pieces together, with only an extra thumb left over, and soon visitors were able to go inside the arm, climb up a winding stairway to the base of the torch and look over the fairgrounds. A painted picture showed everyone how the completed Statue of Liberty would look when it was erected in New York. Meanwhile, from what they could see of it now, fairgoers knew the gigantic statue would be larger than the Colossus of

One of the most unbelievable sights at the Centennial was the hand and torch of a gigantic statue which would be erected in New York Harbor

Rhodes, one of the seven wonders of the ancient world.

Until the huge statue arrived, the largest statue "of modern times" had been the 21½-foot-high *American Volunteer* that stood in front of the Main Exhibition Hall. Most of the statuary arriving for the fair was indoors in the Art Hall, where some pieces had to be kept hidden from the general public. Opening the crates of statues from Europe had revealed a real surprise. Artists from other countries were no longer dressing their statues in Roman togas and Greek draperies. They were not dressed in anything!

Fair directors held hurried conferences behind closed doors to decide what to do with the new art. The paintings from Europe presented the same problem as the statues—no clothes! At last they decided to put everything questionable in the annex of the Art Hall and hang the oversize landscape and battlefield scenes (gory as they were) in the main art galleries. As a result, the only place in the entire fair where the corridors were choked with people was the Art Hall annex.

In the Art Hall was the bronze statue *Emancipation* showing a Negro breaking his chains and a life-size eagle in plaster with half of George Washington (the sculptor had not bothered with legs) on the eagle's back. There were paintings of the German imperial family in warlike poses and a very bloody painting of the Battle of Gettysburg. English paintings had families, landscapes, and pretty ladies. But whole rooms of French paintings were closed to the public. One writer said the nude paintings looked "as if the subjects had been surprised before they had time to dress for the Centennial."

A shockingly lifelike Cleopatra in wax was banished immediately to the annex. She reclined in her royal barge under a golden canopy and was being fanned by a small black slave of wax. But what fascinated the fairgoers was that Cleopatra and her slave moved mechanically. A lazy parrot opened and shut its wings, perching on her finger, while Cleopatra rolled her head and eyes "alluringly." She would have been thrown out at once, but her popularity grew so fast that fairgoers insisted she remain. Finally the fair directors agreed that the public morals must be protected, and one night Cleopatra's barge simply disappeared.

"Photography is not an art," the art committee decided, and so photographs were shown in a special building. There the photographers tried the best way they knew to make their work look like an art. They had posed costumed actors in scenes from well-known paintings. But a photograph of a balcony scene with a badly dressed Romeo and Juliet was not the same as a painting of the pair. The photography building did not attract huge crowds. It was still too difficult for most people to take pictures with a camera.

Closing Day at Centennial City came with a downpour of rain. The fair had built up an unusual attendance record, however. Each month, thousands more had come and by rainy November, there were three times as many people as there had been in the sunny springtime. People covered their heads with handkerchiefs or towels, wore the "impermeables" that were supposed to keep water from their clothes, slipped on their rubberized boots, and came to see the fair close on November 10.

President Grant arrived in a closed carriage for the formal ceremony, which was held at 4 P.M. with only a few people present. Grant's term in office was nearly over, but it would be months before anyone knew whether the next president was to be Hayes or Tilden, since the votes had not yet been counted. Most of the crowd ignored the private ceremonies and went instead to Machinery Hall for a last look at the Corliss. When the huge engine was turned off, they tried to cheer. But the sound that came out was more like a sob than a hurrah. America's first real world's fair was over.

The wreckers came soon after. Europeans marveled that the practical Americans had put together most of the buildings so that they could be taken apart easily and set up somewhere to be used again. Many of the state houses, like Maryland's, returned home again. The Ohio house, built of Ohio stone, still stands and is one of the Fairmount Park Headquarters buildings today. Foreign buildings were sold to private families. Some of the buildings became churches and are still being used. The Swedish schoolhouse was moved to Central Park in New York.

The Art Hall remained and became known as Memorial Hall. By 1969, the building had to be restored and then was rededicated. It is still used by Philadelphia's Fairmount Park Commission. Its dome can be seen from the Schuylkill Expressway—where the traffic that once clogged the Schuylkill River has moved over from water to highway. Horticultural Hall lasted for many years, but finally its glass panes had been broken so often that it was torn down in 1954. One of the fountains, the Catholic Total Abstinence

Fountain, famous for its drinking water that poured over cakes of ice, still stands in its original place.

The Krupp cannon, largest in the world, had been shown proudly by its German makers. They had sold it to the Turkish government for use in the war in Constantinople, but first it was to make a slight detour and appear at the Centennial. The Corliss and the other machines were sent off to work in factories until they were finally outclassed by electric motors and gasoline engines. Then they were scrapped.

Twenty-one freight car loads of exhibits were sent to the Smithsonian Institution. There were so many that a new building had to be constructed for them—the designers made it look very much as the Centennial buildings had looked. One hundred years after the fair, the Smithsonian displayed as many of them as could be found, in the setting of the Centennial type of building. Thousands of people enjoyed the Centennial again during the Bicentennial.

The people of 1876 did not forget the people who would be living during the Bicentennial. They packed a safe with articles and pictures to be opened in 1976.

The Centennial gave Americans a new picture of the rest of the world. But what was more important, the rest of the world saw a new view of America. Until then, most foreign countries knew only what they saw of the United States from our exhibits at a few world's fairs held in Europe. They had not been impressed. America to them was a second-class country, still undeveloped and filled with savage Indian tribes. But Centennial City changed all that. Now a new term came into general use—"American efficiency."

Although the southerners could not afford to take part in the Centennial, they had been watching the results of the successful event. When the suggestion was made to try having a southern fair —to see if it might help the South get back on its feet—there were not too many objections. In 1881, the International Cotton Exposition appeared in Atlanta, Georgia. Two years later, the Southern Exposition was held in Louisville, Kentucky. And the year after that, the World's Industrial and Cotton Centenary Exposition brought crowds of people to New Orleans, Louisiana. Some northerners exhibited at the New Orleans fair. By the time Chicago held a huge fair in 1893, the entire country was breathing more easily because several southern states took part in it.

3
Chicago's "White City"
1893

The World's Columbian Exposition in Chicago inspired everything from the first Ferris wheel and Cracker Jack to the Pledge of Allegiance. The fair was built on land that was a swamp of frozen mud all winter, and when the weather turned warmer it was awash with floods. No one dreamed the swamp could be turned into a fairyland city with elegant white buildings as fancy as wedding cakes, huge white and gold statues, marble arches topped with chariots of gold, and tall white columns set against a deep-blue background of sky and Lake Michigan.

Chicago had grown into a big city with 850 trains a day, three universities, 465 churches, 1,400 hotels, a symphony orchestra, 24 daily newspapers, gaslit streets, elevators in tall buildings, and one large uninhabitable swamp. Yet people along the East Coast still thought of Chicago as the "far west" and not quite civilized. Why else, easterners asked, did Chicago men have three pockets in their suit coats—one for a watch, one for a purse, and the third for a jackknife or revolver?

When a Chicago committee traveled to Washington, D.C., to ask if they might host the fair to celebrate the 400th anniversary of Columbus' landing in the New World, everybody laughed.

"A fair? In that windy city?" joked a New York news writer.

"Who ever heard of a fair so far from the great Eastern seaports?"

But the Chicago group won the right to hold the fair at last, arguing that they did have a seaport of sorts and that it was high time Western folks had a fair of their own. They began at once planning the fair on such a grand scale that it never has had an equal—before or since.

A swamp turned into a fairyland in Chicago at the World's Columbian. The greatest miracle was the incandescent lights at night

The grounds were laid out by Frederick Law Olmsted, America's number one landscape architect. The most famous artists and architects of the United States were gathered together in one room to decide on the fair's appearance. Daniel Burnham, the chief of construction, said to the assembled artisans: "Make no little plans. They have no magic to stir men's blood."

Only the grandest of plans came out of that room. The fair would be called the World's Columbian, but no one thought it would ever be finished in 1892 for the 400th anniversary. The architects had turned thumbs down on the "warehouse" type of barnlike buildings and gingerbready houses that had so excited Centennial visitors. Instead, they decided on classical buildings that would have turned any emperor green with envy—palaces with curlicues, gargoyles, acanthus leaves, towering columns, and statues in niches.

The vote of the architects was not unanimous. Louis Sullivan did his best to talk the group out of the big white elephants. He suggested a more modern, colorful city. He lost the argument, though in the end they told Sullivan he could do his own thing. They gave him the Transportation Building to design any way he wanted, but his building was not to be included in the Court of Honor since it would not match the others. Sullivan was not one to hold his tongue when he had something to say.

"The damage wrought by the World's Fair will last for half a century from this date—if not longer," he grumbled.

He was right. Hundreds of towns across the country built city halls, libraries, and other buildings with tall columns and high narrow windows after the fair. To add insult to Sullivan's insult, the only building to win a prize offered by an important group of French architects was Sullivan's Transportation Building. A young pupil of Sullivan's, Frank Lloyd Wright, was to remember that for many world's fairs afterward.

Besides the artists, other committees were at work with plans. A series of International Congresses were arranged to bring the most brilliant minds of the world to Chicago during the summer. A Congress of Religions brought together for the first time on one stage all the known religions of the world. A Congress on Aerial Navigation predicted that airplanes might someday travel 60 or even 80 miles an hour.

Department Q of the Ethnology Division was charged with the squeamish job of seeing that this fair did not have a shantytown outside its gates as the Centennial and Crystal Palace had. The men of Department Q, working on the principle of "If you can't beat 'em, join 'em," decided to set aside one street that would branch off from the rest of the fair. There they would allow only the most dignified of the shantytown amusements. But the main feature of the street was to be a series of villages of different nationalities, peopled by natives of those countries. The name chosen for the area was "The Midway Plaisance," the French word *plaisance* meaning pleasure of a cultured and dignified sort.

What was most surprising about the pompous White City was the building material. Since it was all to be torn down as soon as the fair ended, the buildings were made of "staff." Staff was a cheap and easily disposable material of plaster of Paris, hemp fiber, and glue. The staff was slapped on over wooden and steel frames, then smoothed (or carved, in the case of statues) and polished until it looked like white marble.

Building the fair along the edge of Lake Michigan during a bone-chilling winter was no picnic. Warm clothing for the laborers included extra suits of scratchy woolen underclothing, scarves, mittens over top of mittens, and hats with earmuffs. The men were so bundled up they could hardly bend over to hammer nails. The artists worked in the few rooms that had been completed enough to be heated by potbellied stoves. As staff was poured for walls, small heaters called "salamanders" were lighted to get the walls dried out. They never did dry completely until the heat of summer came. Slowly, the warmed rooms began to fill up with giant statues —ladies in flowing Grecian robes, vases large enough to hold trees, dolphins and mermaids to sport in the unbuilt fountains.

Outdoors, workmen channeled the ugly swamp water into a design of lakes and canals. Gondolas and singing gondoliers to go with them arrived from Venice. Electric launches that traveled 6 miles an hour were tested on the lakes. A Viking "Dragon Ship," the exact copy of a ship that archaeologists had dug up in Norway, sailed to the New World in 44 days to land eventually on the lake near the Norway Building. The whaling ship *Progress* moved into South Pond before the last arched bridge was built across the water to seal it in.

Wooded Island was created in one lagoon to become a garden of roses and rhododendrons for a Japanese house called "The Phoenix." A picturesque flock of ducks was invited to live among the flowers, but later during the fair there were many complaints that the ducks did not seem to know their place. There were loud outcries when the ducks dropped feathers and other things in front of the Fine Arts Building that faced the North Pond.

Even Lake Michigan was tamed, with a stone wall and a boardwalk along the edge. By the time Opening Day came, the streets that ran from the city to the fair were not finished. But the mud stopped at the gates to the White City.

On Columbus Day in 1892, the fair was dedicated with much ceremony. At the moment of dedication, 12 million schoolchildren stood to recite the Pledge of Allegiance for the first time. The pledge had been written in the offices of *The Youth's Companion,* a magazine for young people. Its editor had felt the need for some sort of patriotic pledge so that Americans could voice their feelings of patriotism. At the same time, the magazine had been campaigning for four years for an American flag to fly over the roof of every schoolhouse in the country.

On May 1, 1893, the World's Columbian was officially opened. Electricity was to be the star of the fair, and it was only right that electric current should help open the fair. When President Grover Cleveland's finger touched a button, the electric fountains turned on, cannons boomed, flags flew up their masts, and the orchestra began playing Handel's "Hallelujah Chorus." The crowd went wild with joy and anticipation.

The fair was so gigantic that people hardly knew where to go first. Trumpets or drums would beckon in one direction only to compete with the jangle of a camel caravan from another way. One tired lady stumbled out of a building and arrived unexpectedly in a strange corner of the grounds. She leaned against a pillar and muttered, "Well, when they planned this fair, they put these buildings so that whenever you come out, you ain't anywhere nearer anything in particular."

At the entrances were fleets of rolling chairs. At first people felt they were only for the sick or aged. But by the second day of the fair, those whose feet already ached were very happy to become riders even though it cost 75 cents an hour. The price was excusable, because the chairs were pushed by nice young men trying to work their way through college. The riders did not realize that the young men were also athletes. Chair pushers from rival colleges sometimes challenged one another to races, with the helpless riders hanging on for dear life.

One of the wonders of the fair was the electric Intramural Railway with 15 trains that carried up to 100 passengers on a 6-mile tour around the outside edges of the fair. The hour-long ride cost 10 cents and at one point the cars sped up to 30 miles an hour! Fair visitors were sure they were witnessing the transportation of the future.

"It suggests a great hereafter," said one rider, "and may even put all those giant locomotives out of business."

People had not been sure whether electricity was going to be a servant of man or just an expensive (and often dangerous) toy.

The World's Columbian was to set the importance of electricity straight in their minds. Crowds stood hypnotized by the Edison Pillar of Light, a tall shaft with 5,000 incandescent bulbs of different colors that winked on and off in patterns. People were thrilled by experiments with artificial lightning, although not sure what it was useful for. A demonstration of cooking by electricity left housewives, who had to go home to their own balky coal stoves, dumbfounded. Edison's Kinetoscope was still another awesome sight—to think that a person might watch pictures that moved!

Even pictures that did not move were still an amazement, because the ordinary person, without heavy cameras and tripods, could now photograph his own family. For $10, anyone could buy one of the new "Kodaks." It was easy to carry and took 48 pictures on a roll of film instead of on glass plates. Unfortunately, the World's Columbian had a stern rule about taking pictures at the fair—the amateur photographer must pay $2 a day, or $5 a week, for the privilege. Later the poor photographer discovered he must pay at almost every one of the foreign villages on the Midway Plaisance. Some "villagers," determined to leave the United States rich, charged as much as 25 cents for each picture. The unlucky camera owner who smuggled his camera into the fair and did not have a tag tied on it to show he had paid the fee could be arrested.

The police inside the fairgrounds were called the Columbian Guard and wore snappy uniforms. Their chief was a former army officer, so they drilled regularly every day on the grounds. They had been on duty since the summer before, while the curious crowd had poured through the gates to supervise the building of the fair. The Guard was in charge of 200 guides (25 of them women) who charged 50 cents an hour for tours. It also had a Secret Service Bureau whose duty was to "clear the grounds of all criminals and bad characters."

The hardest day for the Guards was Chicago Day, October 9, when people began arriving at 6:00 A.M. to stay all day. There were 750,000 visitors, yet only six young men were arrested for disturbance. The Guard book reads on that day, "There were a number of 'toughs,' but they were overawed by the vast preponderance of respectable element and so kept quiet."

The charge for taking photographs was only one of the hidden costs at the fair. Thirsty people had to pay 1 cent a glass for "sterilized water" dipped out of an open cask into an unsterilized

Fairgoers were not encouraged to take their own pictures

glass. Tired people discovered that, if they wanted to sit down, they would have to rent a folding campstool from a concession. No self-respecting person would have flopped down on the ground in 1893. Although admission to the fair was only 50 cents for adults (25 cents for children), a person who wanted to see everything on the Midway Plaisance could easily spend another $40—over two weeks' wages for many hardworking people. Then there were the tempting souvenirs. Ladies bought brooches made to look like the last nail driven into the Women's Building by Mrs. Potter Palmer, the fair's champion of women's rights. There were tortoiseshell combs to wear in the hair, "ever-pointed" pencils, sterling silver Columbus stamp boxes, and the newest idea of all—picture postal cards! Although Europeans had been sending picture postcards, this was America's first chance.

Some of the marvels at the World's Columbian had come to stay and some had not. A young lawyer, Lewis Walker, was fascinated by a hookless fastener that the inventor, W. L. Hudson, was showing. But Hudson had no money to produce his discovery in 1893. Twenty years later, Walker owned the company that gave the zipper to the world. Another young man inspired by the White City was Henry Ford. This was the year he tested his first automobile. In later years, Ford remembered how he had enjoyed the World's Columbian, and his motor company took a part in every fair afterward.

One electrical marvel that evidently did not stay was the Movable Sidwalk that "ran every pleasant day." Everyone who saw it was convinced that this was the way all city dwellers would be traveling to work in the future. The sidewalk was set up on a long pier jutting out into the lake. It was restful, breezy, and cost 5 cents for as long as the rider wanted to stay on. The rider got aboard at a round building where the ride made a circle. There were three platforms—the first was stationary, to help the rider get near the step. The second moved at a walking pace of 3 miles an hour. Then the rider stepped up another inch and a half to the third platform, moving now at 6 miles an hour, and sat down in an easy chair. As the spieler announced loudly, there was "No waiting. No one run over or lost. No noise. No smoke."

One of the rare features at the White City was the largest art exhibition the world had ever seen. Unfortunately, it seems to have been about three times larger than the space available. The statues were packed so close to each other that it was impossible to back away from one without knocking over another. The paintings included some of the most famous art work from all Europe, yet they were hung one above the other. In some places paintings were three and four high, so the art lover's neck fairly creaked from trying to take in pictures hanging from floor to ceiling.

"I am not brazen enough to face some of the pictures I hear are in some of those rooms," one schoolteacher wrote in her diary.

Not everyone felt that way. The world was getting more used to "modern art," but older people still preferred paintings with lots of little cupids and pink ladies wearing clouds of chiffon. They liked Winslow Homer's works, but the sculptor Rodin was shocking. A flock of people collected every day around Thomas Hovenden's painting called *Breaking Home Ties.* It showed a teen-age boy leaving the farm and his family to make his future somewhere else.

Among the outdoor works of art were the Columbian Fountain of Frederick MacMonnies, which stood at one end of the basin, and Daniel Chester French's *Statue of the Republic,* which stood facing it from the other end. In 1893, anything, to be grand, had to be allegorical and tell a story. The statue was huge—her arms were 30 feet long and she was crowned with a ring of electric light bulbs. The fountain was even more huge. Columbus' Barge of State, with the Genius of Discovery directing the vessel, sailed with Fame on the bow, blowing a trumpet while Time steered. It was pulled by four span of seahorses mounted by riders who represented Culture, Intelligence, Heroism, and Truth. But what really impressed the fair visitor was that it cost $100 an hour to operate the fountain when it was lighted at night.

Christopher Columbus himself was represented at the fair with the simplest building of all—the plain little Convent of La Rabida. It was an accurate copy, even down to the vegetation that grew around it. Inside the building was the largest collection of relics of Columbus that Americans have ever seen. Most were returned to Spain when the fair closed and have never been displayed since.

Out in the lake were replicas of the *Niña,* the *Pinta,* and the *Santa María.* They were built in Spain, presented to the United States especially for the fair, and sailed across the Atlantic. They left Palos Harbor in February of 1893 with a Spanish crew and Spanish and American battleship escorts. Now, in Lake Michigan, people could take rides on the *Santa María,* but the old ship lumbered along slowly and did not always turn around when its captain wanted it to.

Every building at the fair had something in it that young people liked especially. The largest building ever constructed by man was the Manufactures and Liberal Arts Building. A magazine writer reported that a ten-story building could be carried through it without touching the sides. The center aisle was so wide it was called Columbia Avenue. In the Machinery Building was a huge crane that traveled the full length of the building. It had been used to carry the heavy machines inside. Now a fence had been put around the crane's wooden floor and for 10 cents people could ride across the building on it, looking down at the machinery beneath. Directly under the dome of the Government Building was a huge hollow section of a sequoia tree, with a winding stairway inside. The Smithsonian exhibit displayed stuffed animals of the North American continent and busts of famous Indian chiefs. It drew huge crowds of people.

Parents could leave young children at the Children's Building while they toured the fair. Upstairs there was a nursery with small fenced-in areas for toddlers (there were no portable playpens then) and bassinets for infants. A "Kitchen Garden" demonstrated ways of teaching preschool children. Even though the kindergarten idea had arrived with the Centennial, in 1893 most people thought of it only as a way to care for poor children whose parents worked during the day. Another schoolroom demonstrated the teaching of deaf children. But the room most young people wanted to see was the gymnasium. In a large room with a balcony there was just about every form of athletic equipment a child could imagine. Attendants cared for many scraped knees and bumped elbows—the results of no soft mats to land on, only the hard floor.

The most unusual building—the only one that did not match—was Louis Sullivan's Transportation Building. He thought architecture should be useful, not ridiculous. From a distance, his building looked like a brilliant picture in a frame. It was pea green with silver trim. The doorway was a dazzling gold with five archways, each decorated with carvings. Best of all, it had a Moorish balcony that became the most popular place at the fair to take a loved one's picture. From this one unharmonious building came the idea for all the buildings when Chicago had its next fair in 1933.

Inside the Transportation Building, people wanted to see the new Pullman cars, designed so they would be easy to clean and with no corners for bedbugs to hide in. The latest in train safety equipment was there, too. A visitor could compare American railroad cars, now made mostly of steel, with the flimsy wooden ones still used for passengers in Europe. On display was the DeWitt Clinton train of 1831 that burned wood for fuel and still traveled at 15 miles an hour in 1893.

Some of the fair was outside in the water, where the most popular exhibit was the battleship *Illinois.* Although it was a fake battleship, built on pilings, it had real guns and was fully manned by a crew of 200 men. A lifesaving show in the water drew huge crowds as the white-jacketed "lifesavers" rescued two people clinging to a fake mast that represented a sunken ship. The crowd never tired of watching the rescued people being hauled ashore by breeches buoy.

Just outside the fence of the fair was Buffalo Bill's Wild West Show. It was not quite refined enough to be allowed inside. The band played so loud that it could be heard well into the center of the fair, just as Buffalo Bill had planned. Visitors to the show bought sour crystallized lemonade drops (there was a souvenir in every package) or 5 cents' worth of popcorn or peanuts, and took their seats in the stands. Buffalo Bill started off the show with Indians, a pony express, and a train attacked by Indians and saved by Cody. But after that, the show had little to do with the Wild West. There were French Cavalry riders, German lancers, Mexican cowboys, British Lancers, Russian Cossacks, and some fast-riding Arabians.

The White City was filled with sounds. For 5 cents, a music lover could put two hard-rubber tubes into his ears, turn on a Graphophone and hear a popular tune, "The Cat Came Back." Sounds of dozens of bands playing music from all over the world added to the din of the Midway Plaisance. Then there was the cry of the

A rare quiet moment in the gym at the Children's Building. Few children had ever seen a gym before

Egyptian lemonade vendor, towel wrapped around his waist, who wandered all over selling his tasteless lemonade out of a strange-looking jug. People paid the 5 cents for a cup just to see how it poured. After the drink, they discovered why he had a towel around his middle—he used it to wipe out the cup before handing it to the next person. The steamboat taking people for rides on the lake had a calliope that played many songs. A machine that weighed people and gave them a fortune plinked out a barely recognizable tune, "In the Sweet Bye and Bye."

All up and down the Midway Plaisance people were bombarded with the "ballyhoo" sounds of the barkers and spielers. The ballyhoo was the words they were saying. People called it "advertising without a conscience," because all along the Midway the truth was greatly exaggerated. The barker was the man whose loud voice called attention to the show inside and got people to stop in their tracks. Then he turned the work over to the spieler, whose job it was to get people to part with their money. He had lungs of tough leather and was a fast-talking salesman, but he was highly paid for his talents.

"We have hootchy-kootchy dancers here," began the spieler. "Not 88 of 'em like they tell you at the other places, but 23. Count 'em." People who took the trouble to count discovered there were actually 14.

"Come in, folks, and see the girls dancing bare!" was one of the spieler's favorite tricks. Once the money was paid and the curious crowd entered, they discovered inside the girls' dancing bear!

The Midway Plaisance brought the world to people who could never have afforded to travel. For 25 cents or less, the Midwesterner could surround himself with all the atmosphere of villages in China, Sudan, Alaska, Tunis and Algiers, the South Sea Islands, Germany, Lapland, Turkey, Persia, and a dozen other countries.

The most exciting spectacle on the Midway Plaisance was the Ferris wheel. Before the fair opened, Burnham's committee had tried to think of some one thing that would do for Chicago what the Eiffel Tower had done for the Paris fair. Someone suggested towers, but Burnham said there was nothing original about a tower. Then a young man, George Washington Gale Ferris, drew a huge wheel on a piece of paper. After several jokes about "the man with wheels in his head" and needing something with more dignity, the committee voted to try Ferris' giant wheel.

*The wondrous Ferris wheel stood in the middle of
the Midway Plaisance*

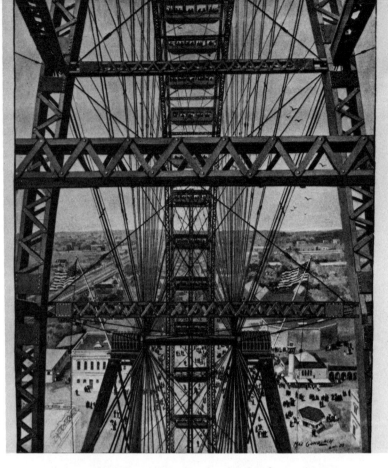

*From the height of the Ferris wheel, riders saw views
that only balloonists had seen before*

Ferris may not have been the first to build a revolving wheel to
carry people. William Somers argued in court that Ferris had seen
his "observation roundabout" in Atlantic City in 1891 and copied
it. There was a long court case, won by Somers, but no one has ever
called it the Somers wheel. At any rate, the wheel built by Ferris
was very much larger.

The Ferris wheel had 36 cars, each holding 60 passengers.
Heavy iron screens covered the windows, and the doors were
locked to make sure that what went up would also come down.
Each revolution took 20 minutes, and a passenger went around
twice for his 50 cents. But people were afraid to try it. The day the
wheel first began to turn, crowds stood on the ground beneath,
completely awestruck. No one volunteered to ride. Most people

thought the sensation of going around would surely make them seasick or dizzy. Then Mrs. Ferris herself offered to ride it. "She showed no fear!" said the newspapers.

Ferris published a pamphlet with pictures of the view that riders would see as they rode around the wheel, and an author drummed up interest in the wheel by writing a story called "Car No. 2, or A Romance of the Ferris Wheel: A Narrative of James Black."

"If your eyes are closed," said Ferris' pamphlet, "you would never know you were going around. At the top, you can see the opposite shores of Lake Michigan, 50 miles away, on a clear day."

The temptations were too much to resist. The passengers paid for the cost of the Ferris wheel within three months. No trip to the fair—or to any fair since 1893—has been complete without a Ferris wheel ride. At the top of the wheel, those first riders were stunned into silent admiration for a view no one except a balloonist had ever seen.

The Ferris wheel, in the middle of the Midway Plaisance, did more than the spieler's ballyhoo to attract people to visit the foreign villages, because the riders could look down and see what was behind the closed fronts. The foreign villages were all that the fair planners had hoped they would be—and a lot more. What Department Q of the Ethnology Division did not know was what a variety of "life" in foreign countries fell under their dignified title. There was everything from belly dancing to cannibalism!

Behind the towers and crenellated walls of an old castle on the Midway was "Ireland." Inside was an authentic copy of the banquet hall in Donegal Castle and a piece of the real Blarney Stone. The tinkling sounds of the bamboo waterwheel greeted visitors to the Javanese village, built of bamboo and woven palm leaves. The unmistakable blare of a German oompah band encouraged people to cross the drawbridge into a feudal village and castle. "Old Vienna" re-created that city as it looked in the year Columbus sailed toward the west. The Laplanders in their village nearly died of the heat, but flocks of people went mainly to see the little baby girl they had christened "Little Bi-lo" after a popular doll.

But the village that packed in the crowds was the Streets of Cairo. For a 10-cent admission, the visitor could completely forget he was in the western hemisphere. The houses inside the walls had wooden grated windows with veiled ladies peering out, balconies

*The only way to describe "Little Egypt's" dancing
was to say she had "educated muscles"*

and archways, walls of lavender and pink, a bazaar filled with
Egyptian souvenirs to buy. An Arab would write a visitor's name
on a card in Arabic for 5 cents. Drivers wearing long caftans and
a fez wandered along with camels and donkeys offering rides for
25 cents. The comic relief of the village was Joseph and his boom-
de-ay donkey. No one could make the donkey move except Joseph. But there was another reason people flocked to the Streets
of Cairo.

"Little Egypt" and her educated muscles was the main attraction. Four years before, a young American boy named Sol Bloom

had gone to the Paris International Exposition and wandered into the Algerian village. There he watched a dance that had been banned in Egypt many years before. Bloom was a promoter of popular entertainment in the states and he bought the exclusive right to show the Algerian dancers, acrobats, glass eaters, and scorpion swallowers at home.

"I doubt very much whether anything resembling the *danse du ventre* was ever seen in Algeria," said nineteen-year-old Bloom, "but I was not at the time concerned with trifles."

In no time *danse du ventre* had been translated into "belly dance," and crowds rushed to see it—all in the interests of ethnology, of course.

Victorians did not part with their money easily—they had worked six full days a week to get it. So when they stopped in front of an amusement like "The Moorish Palace and Its Startling Wonders," they wanted to be sure of getting their 25 cents' worth of entertainment. The visitor walked through a palm garden into a castle that was copied from the Alhambra, with endless colonnades, arches in gold, and bright tiles with views of the Tangier coast through the windows. He visited the harem where the sultan was surrounded by his beauties. But the Victorian fairgoer felt gypped if he was not scared half out of his wits, so a labyrinth led from the harem through a series of terrifying torture scenes and up a pair of steps into a Monster Kaleidoscope where a few people looked like thousands. But that was only the beginning. Another hour was spent going through the Panopticon, a wax museum on the second floor with dozens of scenes and a gallery of important people in wax. If the visitor was not yet totally exhausted, there was the Optical Illusion Theater to see, with three acts of mystifying illusions.

Forty natives of Dahomey had been brought to Chicago to live at the fair and entertain visitors as they danced wildly, brandishing spears and hatchets, to the music of wood drums and iron bells. The Dahomey natives were famous for never having submitted to slavery, killing themselves if captured. They did, however, have to submit to the Purity League, which clothed them in breeches to their knees. They attracted crowds mainly because the barker let it be known they were cannibals who ate their prisoners once a year when they collected the annual tax. The barker assured the crowds that it was not yet tax time in Dahomey.

The Electric Theater attracted large crowds for a performance "that is purely electrical," according to the ballyhoo outside. It was called "A Day in the Alps" and the audience noted a cool breeze (electric fan) inside. First they heard the peasants singing (electric gramophone), then came a storm (there had to be some way to show that lightning!). When the sun came out (an electric light), the audience saw an Alpine village and watched the sun set slowly, leaving the alpenglow on the highest alps (red electric light). Electric stars twinkled in the sky, and then snow began to fall on the village. A performance of this sort was shown for the next several fairs, but added to the scene were floods and fires. At the next fair, the performance was called "The Johnstown Flood." After 1900, it became "The Galveston Flood," and after 1913 it was "The Dayton Flood."

The baby incubators had been invented by Dr. Couney as a way to keep very tiny babies alive until they could survive in the world. Until his incubators, there had been almost no hope for babies born too small or too soon to live.

"Is it worth it?" asked a sign outside the concession, because people believed that children could not be normal if they were too small at birth. "Julius Caesar and Balzac were born too small," the sign continued.

When a visitor was filled with learning from the fair and the Midway Plaisance, there were some rides just for fun. The Ice Railway was one—like a toboggan ride, for 10 cents. The customer received a handful of snow after the ride. The Barre Sliding Railway had cars that were moved very quickly and silently along a one-mile track by jets of water. Another of the wonders was the first ice-skating rink on artificial ice—no one had ever before skated in the summer.

"Night is the magician of the fair," said everyone who had ever been there when the sun went down, leaving the buildings momentarily in darkness. After the fireworks came the magic of the fair lighted up at night with incandescent bulbs. Electric "sunbeams" placed on high towers lighted up the domes and tops of the tallest buildings. Inside the dome of the Administration Building were 5,000 light bulbs. Other buildings had rows of light bulbs outlining them against the black sky. Except for the electric fountains, which had colored lights shining on the jets of water, all the lights at the fair were white. Crowds oohed and ahhed at the sight

—too entranced by the bright lights to do more than walk around to see the views from every angle.

Then came the night of October 28. It was United Cities Day and the mayor of Chicago, Carter Harrison, had been invited to speak.

"Chicago was only a swamp when I came into the world," he said. "I expect to live half a century more, when Chicago will be more of a metropolis than New York."

His speech brought cheers of expectation from Chicagoans who were tired of large Eastern cities making fun of the Midwest. But the mayor's time had run out. He was shot and killed that night at his own front door by a "demented office seeker."

At the White City, the crowds heard the announcement of the mayor's death quietly. Flags were lowered to half-mast and the orchestra played the funeral march. There was a 21-gun salute at sunset and the great World's Columbian Exposition was closed forever. People walked out of the gates silently—it was hard to believe the fair would all be gone tomorrow.

Some people paid the 25-cent admission to watch the wreckers reduce the buildings to plaster dust. Only one was left standing—the Fine Arts Building became the Field Columbian Museum. Then, in the late 1920's, at a cost of $10 million, it was completely rebuilt and opened again in 1931 as the Museum of Science and Industry.

Much of the World's Columbian was loaded onto freight cars and transplanted to San Francisco. There it formed the basis for the huge California Midwinter Exhibition of 1894 and helped pull the state out of a depression.

The Ferris wheel was used in a Chicago amusement park for a while, then sent to St. Louis for the 1904 fair. The Delaware State Building was bought, loaded onto a barge and taken through Lake Michigan down the Wolf River (they were connected then), where it was plopped down on a good-looking plot of ground without even permission from the owners of the land. It finally crumbled from neglect in 1943. Iowa's building was a popular meeting place for a few years, but it was torn down in 1936.

The foreign buildings traveled different directions, too. The Norwegian Building was bought by the Wrigley family and shipped to Lake Geneva, where it became a card-playing pavilion, then a motion picture theater. Finally it was given to Little Norway, Wisconsin. Ceylon Court, the beautiful Singhalese Temple, was sold for $2,000 and shipped to Lake Geneva on 23 freight cars to be used as a summer home. The Wooded Island was still a lovely garden 40 years later, kept in shape by one of the German gardeners who became head landscaper. The Japanese "Phoenix House" survived on Wooded Island until World War II when vandals burned it to the ground.

Chicago still has Jackson Park along the lakefront to show that a fair passed by that way. The great *Statue of the Republic* was torn down because she was built of staff but a smaller replica of her still stands today at the foot of 65th Street.

Most of the results of the White City could not be measured with yardsticks. The Midway Plaisance had brought so much pleasure that no fair would ever be held again without some sort of amusement area. Travel to and from the fair left its improvements, too. For the first time, round-trip prices were established, and so were long-distance trains without sleeping cars for people who could not afford Pullmans. Artificial ice rinks were built in many cities. As Sullivan had warned, the "wedding cake" architecture was repeated for at least another thirty years. A large group of devoted fairgoers formed "The '93ers." Their purpose was to keep alive the World's Columbian for at least as long as they lived. One of the carpenters who was paid a dollar a day working to tear down the White City managed to excite his son in later years with tales of the fabulous fair. The carpenter was Elias Disney, whose son, Walt, would play a very important part in future fairs.

The World's Columbian started an epidemic of fairs. The first one to follow was San Francisco's California Midwinter Exposition. Much of the Chicago fair was loaded onto freight cars and shipped west for the fair that was to help get California out of a severe depression. The year after that, another International Cotton Exposition in Atlanta, Georgia, featured cotton plants from all over the world and stressed trade with Latin-American countries. For the first time since the Civil War, black people had a separate exhibit to show their achievements and progress. The Liberty Bell traveled to this fair, drawing thousands of southerners who just wanted to touch the symbol of liberty—at last the Civil War was finally over.

Omaha, Nebraska, an important U.S. city, had a huge fair in 1898 to show the rest of the country that the people on the western side of the Mississippi River had industries and civilization, too. During this Trans-Mississippi Exposition, called the "Magic City," an important Congress of Indians met.

Buffalo, New York, became known as the "Electric City" after the Pan-American Exposition in 1901. All the electricity used for the "Pan" came from Niagara Falls. On the eve of the building of the Panama Canal, this fair was meant to promote relations between North, South, and Central America.

Charleston, South Carolina, joined the other fair cities in 1902 with a large fair intended to increase trade with the West Indies —the South Carolina and West Indian Exposition. Fairs were contagious, and soon the city of St. Louis, Missouri, had a special reason for a fair of its own.

4

St. Louis' "Ivory City"
1904

The summer of 1904 was an inspiring time to be young. The Wright brothers had just proved that man could really hope to fly in the air someday in something more dependable than a balloon basket. Sound could travel through the air without wires. Nearly every teen-ager living in a big city had seen at least one motorcar. And phonograph records were now playing the new music called ragtime.

Young people who lived near St. Louis, Missouri, were the most excited of all. The Louisiana Purchase Exposition, to commemorate the 100th anniversary of the opening up of the West, was to open on April 30. The fair would be twice as large as the World's Columbian in Chicago and would cost twice as much. Although the city had only a 650-acre park to put the fair in, the planners found they might double the area by using the buildings (not yet occupied) and grounds that would someday belong to Washington University, adjoining the park.

Everything about the St. Louis fair was an attempt to outdo the one in Chicago. For the first time, fairgoers would see not only man and his products but also how he made those products. Shoes would be made, metals smelted, and even armor-piercing shells would be demonstrated before the startled eyes of the visitors.

The buildings were tinted ivory—much easier on the eyes than those glaring-white Chicago buildings that nearly blinded the poor fairgoers who did not wear smoked glasses on sunny days. The lights at night were not even to be compared with Chicago's. While visitors there had been thrilled at the mere sight of a bare light bulb hanging at the end of an electric wire, the St. Louis fair had lights that rarely exposed a bulb.

St. Louis had International Congresses, as Chicago did. But it went one step farther and invited the Olympic Games to be held for the first time in the United States. Only eight years before, the First Olympiad in Athens, Greece, had revived the ancient Greek games. Four years before, the Olympics had been held in Paris, France. St. Louis built a huge athletic field, a stadium, and a granite gymnasium (later to be turned over to Washington University) for the Olympics that were held August 29 to September 3.

While Chicago had only held an International Congress on Aeronautics, St. Louis thought it quite possible that the Wright brothers' flight had opened a new era in transportation. They

A group of young people stop on the porch to pose for a picture before setting off for the fair, complete with picnic basket

immediately added an "aeronautic concourse" to the fairgrounds to bring all sorts of flying machines to St. Louis. They offered $100,000 in prizes to any airship (balloon, dirigible, or anything else that flew) that could make the best record of flying over a prescribed course at a speed of not less than 20 miles an hour. The prescribed course was what made the contest difficult. Almost anyone could take an airship up into the air and bring it down again, but to make it go where the pilot wanted it to go was a real feat. It was the first great air contest ever held.

St. Louis fair managers did not see why the amusement zone had to be educational and pretend to be a branch of the anthropological department. They reasoned there was nothing wrong with having fun. But the Ladies Purity League reasoned differently. They handed the amusement committee some demands—no spielers (barkers were all right), no peddling of junk, and above all, no indecent dancing, no matter how authentic it was in other countries. The committee had to agree. Then they found a Frederic Remington sculpture of four cowboys riding into town for a rip-roaring good time and put it at the gates to the amusement area.

Early in 1903 everyone realized the fair would never be built in time for the centennial of the Louisiana Purchase, so the opening was put off until the next summer. But a huge dedication day was held on May 1, 1903, to build up excitement for the event to come. Henry Pain, the fireworks king, spent $55,000 on three hours of smoke and noise such as no one had ever experienced. The sensation of the evening was seven gas balloons rising above the ground at one time. Each was controlled by a skilled aeronaut —the new breed of hero for audiences. The aeronauts fired a salute of aerial guns, then released giant flags of the six greatest nations taking a part in the "Universal Exposition." The seventh balloon dropped an American flag made of flaming fireworks—it was 400 feet long! On the ground, a set piece of fireworks created a sneak preview of what the fair's most famous Festival Hall with its Cascade Gardens would look like. It was only the palest hint of the elegant city that the impatient crowd would be seeing a year later.

After dedication day, the excited people went home to wait for the opening day a year later. During the year they wondered what lay ahead. There was talk of a motorcar that held twenty people at once to tour the fairgrounds, and of a parade of motorcars through the city streets that would surely panic every horse in town. Mr. Edison promised something more exciting than the phonograph. People only hoped there would not be another tragedy like the one at the last fair, in Buffalo in 1901. In the Festival Music Hall, the President of the United States, William McKinley, had been shot by an anarchist. McKinley had died eight days later.

During the long winter, the young people of St. Louis entertained themselves by watching the Ivory City rise on rolling land that had once been only farms and trees. The pompous buildings, every bit as fancy as Chicago's, were made of staff that used manila fibers. The tough fibers came from the Philippine Islands, now under the protection of the United States.

Young people who were allowed to touch cards played games such as "It," "Jonah," and a new game called "Election," advertised as "free from the objections to most cards and would not damage young morals."

Another advertisement read, "A phonograph is the only infallible amusement for every sort of visitor." The machine had to be wound up for each record, so the music began quite fast, slowing to a crawl before someone wound up the machine again. Ragtime music was almost guaranteed to drive the older folks up the wall. "Under the Bamboo Tree" and Scott Joplin's "Cascade Rag" (written for the fair) were the most popular. Adults would have preferred sentimental tunes like "Sweet Adoline" or "Idah, Sweet as Apple Cidah" or the thrilling voice of Enrico Caruso. Soon a new song would be on everyone's lips—"Meet Me in St. Louis, Louis . . . meet me at the fair . . ."

Boys were all reading *The Adventures of Buffalo Bill* when they could get it away from their fathers. Girls liked books about the "new woman." One of these was *The Singular Miss Smith*, the story of a wealthy girl who cannot imagine why it is hard to find a maid, so she gets a job as a domestic to see what it's like. She falls in love with a foundry worker who turns out to be a Harvard professor also experimenting with life among the working classes. *The Motor Pirate* was one of the first books written about motorcars. The "pirate" drove a machine powered by liquid hydrogen which traveled at unheard of speeds. He robbed and killed, eluding detectives, until justice triumphed in the end.

A good salary in 1904 was $12 a week. Young men were happy

[ILLUSTRATION ON PRECEDING TWO PAGES]
In an ivory-tinted wonderland, fair visitors discov-
ered the wonders of wireless telegraphy, colored
lights, and the ice-cream cone

because the safety razor had been invented, but their fathers went
on sharpening their old-style razors every few minutes while shav-
ing, just as they always had. Ladies were excited about the new
rayon, an artificial silk material, but men had discovered "the
bachelor undershirt," which had no buttons. Instead, it had a neck-
band that stretched, and it cost 50 cents. Many years later it would
be called the T-shirt.

The long winter ended on April 30, 1904. Delighted crowds
heard John Philip Sousa's band play and a chorus sing "Hymn of
the West," written especially for the fair. The star of this fair was
to be the wireless telegraph, but the old telegraph key was used
to signal the opening. The fair's president, David R. Francis,
touched a telegraph key to alert President Theodore Roosevelt in
Washington, D.C. Then the President pressed his telegraph key
and the fountains shot up their spray and 10,000 flags suddenly
rose to flutter from their masts.

The Universal Exposition was an ivory-tinted fairyland. The
River des Peres had been tamed into a series of lakes and canals
on which floated all sorts of boats—gondolas, swan boats, peacock
boats, dragon-shaped boats, electric and steam launches. The
beautiful Festival Hall, with a dome larger than St. Peter's in
Rome, made such a splendid scene with its cascading waterfalls
that the architects of the fair had called it "the main picture." The
Main Picture, including the most beautiful buildings, was spread
out in a fan shape over gently rolling landscaped hills.

Visitors entered through new automatic turnstiles that did not
open unless a 50-cent coin was put in the slot. Once inside, they
could walk, or hire roller chairs, jinrikshas, or zebu carriages, or
ride on burros, elephants, or camels. An electric streetcar line took
the people through the grounds, while the younger ones piled
aboard the sight-seeing automobiles.

Inside the gates, people headed in all directions. Some wanted
to see the Smithsonian's Bird Cage first—a gigantic outdoor aviary

where the birds could fly almost as free as in nature. Others took their children to see the giant Floral Map, so they could walk around the borders of the states and see the variety of flowers and vegetables that grew within each state. The "meeting place" for families and friends to get together was usually the giant Floral Clock made entirely of living plants. The numbers on the clock were twelve feet long, its hands weighed over a ton, and around its dial were plants that opened their blossoms at different hours of the day.

At the Government Building, people asked to see the wireless telegraph that was click-ck-ck-ing away. They could understand how a telegraph could work with wires strung out from city to city across the country. But this one—without wires—was hard to fathom.

Finally, one man who had asked for an explanation, shrugged his shoulders and remarked, "We don't want to run the thing ourselves. All we want is a few general ideas that can be got without sweating."

There were two systems of wireless telegraphy—the Marconi system and the De Forest system. In 1902, a wireless message had been sent from England to Cape Cod by the Marconi system, using dots and dashes. De Forest was more interested in trying to send voice sounds over the wireless. At the fair, De Forest had put up a very tall steel tower and immediately visitors discovered that it offered the best view of the fair. All around the De Forest station were "numerous long fine wires" waving in the air. They were "antennae," a new word to Americans. Every hour press releases were sent to cities around the United States from the tower.

Sending voice sounds over the wireless was called "wireless telephony" at first. In the court of the Electrical Building, this wonder was demonstrated dramatically. Two huge searchlights, each with a curved mirror behind the light, were set 500 feet apart so their beams met. At night the sounds traveled over the beam of light. A person holding an ordinary telephone receiver and standing at the base of one of the great lights could hear sounds from a phonograph record being played at the base of the other light. It was a great piece of showmanship, but needed quite a bit of working on before the development of "radio telephony." In three more years, after some important inventions such as the De Forest triode vacuum tube and the Fessenden improved transmitter, a new word—radio—would be on everyone's mind.

Other electrical wonders collected the crowds as well. Everyone wanted to see how the telephone switchboard worked. The operator in front of her huge board covered with lights was an immediate heroine for thousands of little girls who wanted nothing more than to be telephone operators. Already, though, she was being replaced by automatic telephone exchanges in some parts of the country. Some cities even had dial telephones with numbers from 1 to 9 on the dial. Instead of the operator ringing the telephone in someone's house, the person who had dialed the number had a button to press and could ring the bell.

Some of the electrical machines that drew admiring audiences in the Ivory City never did become important. Such a failure was the telautograph machine—an improved version of one that appeared in Chicago in 1893. With it, a person could send an order in his own handwriting to a company over twenty miles away. But its inventor, Professor Gray, was to learn that in years to come, people's handwriting grew worse and typewriters became better. No one ever really needed his telautograph.

Electricity had become more and more necessary to people's comfort since the Chicago fair. Flatirons, sewing machines, and stoves that worked electrically had been developed. But they had to be attached directly to electric wires brought into a home. Until 1904 no one had invented a simple electrical attachment wall plug so that a person who wanted to use the iron or other appliance could just plug it into a wall outlet.

Many fair visitors were from the Midwestern states and had never even seen electric lights. For them, the Ivory City lighted at night was something never to be forgotten. One visitor wrote down this description in his diary:

"There is nothing sudden about turning on and off the lights at night. First a faint dim glow is noticed. It slowly increases. They are shut off in the same way, growing dimmer and dimmer until only a dull red glow is visible. The last glow dies away and there is darkness."

Incandescent light bulbs were used to outline the buildings and some of the statues at night. Most of the bulbs were hidden behind shrubbery where they could highlight the flagpoles, lampposts, obelisks, bridges, and building entrances. Globes of different colors were used to create new effects. The cascading waterfalls be-

fore the Festival Hall were all lighted in red one week, in green
another, and yellow another time.

People came to the fair as they would to a circus. Before they
left home, families had made lists of attractions they did not want
to miss—without any notion of how far they must walk to see
everything on the list. Somehow, most people managed to survive
and still see the most popular items on their lists—the Boer War,

The Main Picture at night had colored waterfalls cas-
cading gracefully down in front of Festival Hall

a concert on the world's largest organ, the seals in the Fisheries Building, the fancy rifle exhibit, the Olympic Games, lectures on radium and on wireless telegraphy, the exhibit of paintings, Hale's Breathtaking Firefighters, and the ancient Mexican city of Mitla. They signed the visitors' book in their own state building and visited the Philippines.

One of the criticisms of the fair was that there was just too much to see. One man halted in front of the new light for a lighthouse and was explaining it to his children when another man arrived with his family.

"What's that?" his tired wife asked.

"An engine headlight."

"No, sir," said the first man. "That is a lighthouse."

"Is that so?" said the first, with only a glimmer of interest. "Jane, that's a lighthouse. Now let's get lunch."

The Philippines Exposition was so large it was a fair all by itself. The Spanish-American war, only recently ended, had left the Philippine Islands and the island of Puerto Rico under the protection of the United States. In the Philippines there was still guerrilla fighting. Americans could not understand why the Filipinos, since their country was still filled with savages, were not delighted to be taken under the wing of the United States but preferred to be independent. The curiosity of Americans about their new countrymen was not eased by the tales that came out of the Philippines Exposition in the Ivory City.

One of the tribes at the fair, the Igorots, had a taste for eating dogs, which they satisfied by bribing young boys to catch stray dogs for them. (They had a preference for black dogs.) The Society for the Prevention of Cruelty to Animals was very upset, and so were a large number of dog owners. Other people asked what was the difference. Americans ate pigs, cows, and lambs, why shouldn't the Igorots eat dogs? Finally, a complaint was made to the President of the United States. Theodore Roosevelt wrote back that the Igorots were our guests and their appetites had to be appeased somehow.

Fair visitors, including dog lovers, flocked to the 47 acres that held the Philippines Exposition. Morning was the best time, because then most of the natives were engaged in water sports on the lake. Visitors crossed over The Bridge of Spain and entered the walled city of Manila, made realistic by including copies of Manila's famous landmarks. The best displays of Filipino arts and crafts ever seen by Americans were shown there. Natives sold braided palm-leaf hats, plaited mats, wood carvings, and other handiwork. A large restaurant sat among the fields of rice, sugarcane, tobacco, drying copra, cotton, and manila plants.

All around Manila were small villages, each housing a different tribe in its own native style of house. The only unnative touch was the britches that the Ladies Purity League made the men wear. A Moro village of houses on bamboo poles extended out into the lake, where the villagers could fish and dive for pearls. The Moros were Mohammedan, but some of the Filipinos, like the Tagalogs, Visayans, and Mestizos, were Christian. Some, like the Igorots and the Negritos, were pagan. Many people watched the Negritos, who were such experts with the bow and arrow that the fair managers asked them to help reduce the number of sparrows nesting in the trees. Even the Igorots came in three varieties—the Suyon Igorots who were miners and metalworkers, the Tingiane Igorots who were agricultural, and the Bontoc Igorots who were headhunters—but willing to settle for dogs.

An illogical note at the Philippines Exposition was one tiny building belonging to Puerto Rico. Since those islanders also spoke Spanish and had come under the protectorate of the United States at the same time as the Philippines, it did not seem strange to the fair managers to lump them together, even though they lived thousands of miles apart and had nothing in common.

Many foreign countries had their own buildings in the fairgrounds, far from the area set aside for the Philippines. Japan had a copy of a palace in Tokyo with tea pavilions and a pagoda. Holland had a typical gabled Dutch house with a famous Rembrandt painting that could be seen for an additional 10-cent fee. China re-created Prince Pu Lun's country home, brightly colored in scarlet, ebony, blue, and gold trim. Germany had a copy of the Charlottenburg Castle, and fair visitors admired its hourly chimes and a huge bronze eagle of 5,000 bronze feathers each made separately. Replicas of the Grand Trianon of Versailles and Queen Marie Antoinette's favorite chalets were built by France. Belgium had the only building without windows—remarkable in 1904, but a coming trend in fairs.

Some of the wonders inside the fair appealed to hungry visitors. When the ice-cream salesman ran out of plates one day, he borrowed some waffles from a neighboring booth. Rolling them up into a cone shape, the man was surprised to discover how appealing they were. He had just invented America's most popular treat —the ice-cream cone. Another surprised inventor was the hot tea salesman who could not make any sales in St. Louis' steamy summer weather. He finally poured his tea over crushed ice, and people liked it better than they had ever liked hot tea. Fruit icicles, frozen in long, narrow tins, were much less popular with parents who had to wash up sticky children when the icicles melted. A sausage salesman discovered great popularity for his sausages when he put them inside a bun and called them "hot dogs."

The Agricultural Palace could boast the world's largest rose garden as well as desert, wild flower, and water gardens. One of the most admired plants in the water garden was the water hyacinth. Perfectly proper ladies (who would never dream of stealing) were not above a quick kneebend, a hand plunged into the water, and a hyacinth quickly concealed in a handbag. Thus transported to streams all around the country, the water hyacinths spread happily until they choked dozens of small streams to death with their thick roots. Now, seventy-five years later, the water hyacinth is on the list of plants that are endangering the ecology.

The Art Palace finally concentrated on American artists, although other countries were represented. Whistler's *Rosa Corder* was the most popular American painting, some guidebooks going so far as to say the study of that painting alone was worth the trip to St. Louis. The same problem of skimpy (if any) clothing on the models was repeating itself. A popular French painting called *Flower of the Harem* had won a prize in Paris' 1900 exhibition. But in St. Louis it rated only the comment: "The feller that did that one wasn't the kind ye'd want yer sister to know."

The flocks of people who had stood in motionless awe before the huge locomotives in Chicago now gave only a glance at the world's largest engine on a turntable in the Transportation Building, its powerful wheels churning realistically with compressed air. Nor was the building itself, the size of 9 football fields, getting much attention. The audiences were heading toward the exhibit of 160 different kinds of motorcars—run by gas, electric power, and steam power.

Everywhere they went in the fairgrounds they could hear the

"taut-taut" of the chauffeur's horn. There was everything from the Olds standard runabout (for $650) to a car that had silk curtains, an armchair, a writing desk, a movable washbasin, an icebox, and a closet (for $18,000). Packard cars had a new slot gearshift, and the newest improvements were quick demountable tire rims and the steering wheel principle whereby the car could turn a corner without turning the whole axle. (Automobiles still did not have front bumpers, left-hand steering, electric self-starting, nonskid tires, or all-steel bodies.)

People who wanted to risk riding in an electric or steam automobile had a chance to tour the fairgrounds in motorcars that held from 2 to 60 people. The one car that seated 20 people boasted a chauffeur who was "a living guidebook." In addition, the authorities in the Transportation Building had this to say about it:

"This is the machine that will occupy a place at the great International Exposition of 1950 in the historic automobile exhibit as the crude beginning of a great invention."

They were wrong.

On August 27, St. Louis was the scene of the greatest motor parade ever seen in the world. Cars had been driven from as far away as New York for the event. Every car was decorated with flowers. Some had "wireless poles" attached so they could pick up messages sent out from the De Forest tower.

At the fair that summer were people whose names would be heard again. Helen Keller, a senior at Radcliffe College, went with her teacher, Miss Anne Sullivan. One of the ballyhoo men along the Pike was especially good at twirling a rope, but rather shy when it came to words—his name was Will Rogers. Max Factor, who had learned the art of makeup in the court of the czar, was there. But "nice people" did not use makeup, so the man who was to make his fortune in lipstick and rouge would have to wait for the moving pictures to change things. A singing waiter in the Irish Village, John McCormack, would become famous very soon. Meanwhile, a New York City woman (nameless) made an appearance at the fair in a pants suit and was not allowed in the ladies' lounge.

Moving pictures were on the way. Thomas Edison had perfected the first sound pictures with his Cameraphone, but it would be many more years before fairgoers would actually see such a wonder. Right then, they were happy with the first film story, called *The Great Train Robbery*. They did not need sound. A pianist in the front of the theater supplied continuous music, and the audience supplied every other sound that was needed—hisses, boos, and cheers. All around the fair were 1-cent peep shows that showed "movies" of another sort to one person at a time. The viewer bent over and looked into a machine at hundreds of "still" pictures that had been posed. As the pictures flipped fast, the actors in them appeared to be moving.

One of the popular places to see was the railroad post-office car. In order to speed the mails, mail was sorted (called "throwing the mails") while the post-office car sped along the track between cities. A favorite part of the exhibit was "Owney," the postal clerk's dog (now stuffed). Owney had walked onto a post-office car one day and evidently decided that was the life for him. He traveled thousands of miles, belonging to no one postal clerk in particular. After he died, his body was stuffed and Owney was still traveling—to fairs.

Fairs have always been a place for people to study "model cities." In a way, each fair was a model city itself. Now, in St. Louis, a real Model City was created; its railroad station was one of the entrances to the fair. People were realizing that their cities were developing unpleasant slums. The Ivory City's Model City was built to show how careful city planning could eliminate some of the mistakes that happened in cities that just grew in helter-skelter fashion. But there were troubles in the Model City. Its main street was called Muddled Street, an un-model restaurant sneaked into the town, and the model plaza soil absolutely refused to grow any sort of living thing. In the city, many U.S. cities showed what they believed to be best in their own city—New York had models of its subway system and public library. Other cities showed ways to combat smoke nuisance, incinerate garbage, use scows for dumping garbage into the ocean, and build public bath places. One of the best ideas the fair had for a model city, said most people, was to have outdoor restaurants like the one in the Tyrolean Alps along the Pike.

The Pike was the amusement area, well-marked by the statue of the cowboys which caused much controversy. Sculpture, said the "experts," should be in repose and create a monumental effect. It should never be a "picture." One sculptor, jealous of the popularity of the cowboys statue with younger audiences, grumbled about "the undignified little horses and the cowboys throwing their bodies and arms about and shooting off revolvers into the air." Another complained "that clutter of 16 pony legs makes an absurd underpinning to a monumental group." In spite of the critics, young artists were happy to see sculptors getting away from the statues of Americans wearing Roman togas.

In spite of the watchful eyes of the Ladies Purity League, there was fun on the mile-long Pike. Some amusements were brand-new, others were updated from previous fairs. The Observation Wheel, as high as a 25-story building, was the same Ferris wheel that had delighted so many fairgoers in 1893.

"Creation" was part amusement, part Sunday school lesson. The visitor moved through underground passages in a boat, past Biblical scenes, until he left the boat in a roomy cavern. He weaved up and down stairs, past illusions such as living heads

A rip-roarin', rootin'-tootin' statue shocked visitors who still thought of American statuary as people wearing Roman togas

without bodies, and finally into an auditorium where he heard the music of Haydn's "Creation" and saw pictures of the creation of the earth on stage.

"The Hereafter" was another Sunday school lesson, masquerading as fun. It was a solemn and gruesome show, based on Dante's *Inferno* and designed to scare the living daylights out of children. The visitor was steered by a guide past ghosts who grabbed at him. Then he was rowed across the river of Death, appearing before

The fun place to go in 1904 was the Pike, where amusement was not necessarily educational

the throne of Minos, one of the three judges of the lower world. The guide led the terrified visitor past demons, wicked people who were frozen yet were alive, people who were burning, and into the throne room of Satan, where demons leaped and flew at them. Far from having a Parental Guidance rating, this show was a favorite place for Sunday school teachers to take their classes.

One of the favored attractions at the Chicago 1893 Fair had been "A Day in the Alps." Now the same gimmicks were used to depict "The Galveston Flood." At the Buffalo fair, crowds had thrilled to "The Johnstown Flood," but according to the advertisements "all the gruesome scenes were omitted and only the terrible beauty of the catastrophe" was shown with all the pandemonium and terrifying effects that electricity could produce. Another old favorite was the baby incubators, still doing business.

"Under and Over the Sea" took people for a ride on two of the world's most modern inventions, the submarine and the airship. On the underwater trip to Europe, visitors each had a porthole to look out of and see the wonders to be found at the bottom of the ocean—sunken ships, sea monsters, and Davy Jones's Locker. After they arrived in Paris, they ascended the Eiffel Tower, then stepped into the huge basket of an airship. They survived a terrible storm while crossing the ocean, and finally arrived safely back at the Mississippi River, where they could look down from the balloon and see the Ivory City at St. Louis.

By the time the fair closed on December 1, everyone knew that Theodore Roosevelt would be President for another four years. America was enjoying peace, and work on the Panama Canal was beginning. People went home from the fair with new ideas, new hopes, and souvenirs such as little plates made of a new material called aluminum and a watch with the Main Picture painted on the face.

Closing Day was called "Francis Day," named for the president of the exposition.

"I am about to perform a heart-rending duty," said David R. Francis, as he turned off the lights of the Ivory City. In the darkness, the band played "Auld Lang Syne." Then there was an explosion of elegant fireworks, and the fair was over. Demolition began the next day. Visitors paid 25 cents to watch, but eventually they watched free, when there was no longer anyone to take tickets.

Some of the exhibits were sent on freight cars to Portland, Oregon, to be seen again at the Lewis and Clark Exposition in 1905. Mountains of crushed staff were used for landfill. The lake was reshaped somewhat, and 75,000 trees were planted behind the Art Palace, which was one of the buildings to stay. Several of the statues were kept, but some were eventually lost. Two statues were recast in marble, and one, the statue of St. Louis, was recast in bronze.

Many state buildings were sold to families for private homes for only a few hundred dollars each. New Mexico's was sent to Santa Fe to become a public library there. The Swedish building traveled to Kansas to become the Art Department of Bethany College. Brazil's White Palace was sent back to Rio de Janeiro and rebuilt there. Maine's hunting lodge was moved to the Ozarks, where it became part of a private school. The Japanese pavilion became a bandstand at Forest Park Highlands amusement park. It was destroyed by fire in 1963. The "Orangery" of Great Britain, a copy of the one built by Christopher Wren in Kensington Gardens, became a part of Washington University, as did some of the athletic fields and the gymnasium built for the Olympics.

Alabama's statue of Vulcan, which was so large that a horse and buggy could be driven between its legs, was returned to that state and dumped on a mountain, where it lay until the Alabama State Fair gave it a home. In 1939 it was set up on Red Mountain, near Birmingham, as a monument to the city's steel heritage.

The largest organ in the world and the huge German bronze eagle were bought by John Wanamaker in Philadelphia for his department store. The organ was made even larger through the yeas and is still played daily for shoppers. The eagle became a famous symbol and a meeting place for visitors to Wanamaker's.

The insides of the Model City's model drugstore were bought by a Boston druggist and used by him until he retired in 1977. They are now back in St. Louis in storage waiting for use in a museum.

One of the hardest portions of the fair to get rid of was the Pike. They could not give away the concessions, let alone sell them. For a while people thought another Coney Island would be made out of the Pike, but Washington University was not happy to have it in its front yard. The Ferris wheel, not at all as popular as it had been in Chicago, was torn apart and the pieces sold for scrap.

St. Louis still has its Forest Park as a remembrance of the fair as well as the Art Palace, the New Hampshire House, the giant

Bird Cage, the statute of St. Louis and the statues flanking the entrance to the Palace, the Jefferson Memorial Building (where the Missouri Historical Society and the Library are now), and the World's Fair Pavilion that was built in 1908 on the site where the Missouri Building had burned to the ground two weeks before the fair closed.

Seventy years after the fair closed, a group of senior citizens—all of whom had been at the fair—returned to the scene. Walter told how he had peddled newspapers beside the Floral Clock, doubling the price to 2 cents inside the fairgrounds. William was ten when the fair was torn down. He had earned 25 cents an hour pulling nails out of wood. His father had died the year before and William needed money. He had also earned some money collecting stray dogs for the Igorots.

No sooner had the St. Louis fair closed than a new fair opened in Portland, Oregon. The American Pacific Exposition, better known as the Lewis and Clark Centennial, was to celebrate the 100th year since explorations had begun in Oregon country.

Not to be outdone by a mere centennial, the town of Hampton Roads, Virginia, opened the Jamestown Ter-Centennial in 1907 to mark the 300th year since the founding of the first English-speaking colony in the New World. Two years later, a fair in Seattle, Washington, shared honors with all the nations bordering the Pacific Ocean when the Alaska-Yukon Pacific Exposition opened.

Even though San Francisco had planned to have an important fair in 1915, the town of San Diego, California, also had plans. It copied important Spanish buildings, such as the Alhambra, for an unusually beautiful Panama-California Exposition. The San Diego fair concentrated on natural history and the San Francisco fair featured culture and the arts.

5

San Francisco's "Jewel City" 1915

A pale-pink dream city with a Tower of Jewels that shimmered in the sun and sparkled at night by the light of a man-made aurora borealis—that was the Panama-Pacific International Exposition in San Francisco, California. The lights at night were so bright that some scientists suspected they had attracted attention on Mars and the Martians were trying to get in touch with this planet.

The fair, called the P.P.I.E. for short, was to celebrate the opening of the Panama Canal. San Franciscans hoped the Canal was going to make their city every bit as busy as New York. But they had another reason for wanting to host a fair. Only nine years before, a disastrous earthquake and fire had almost put San Francisco out of business forever. The fair was their way of showing the world that their city was alive and well. The only space large enough for a fair was on land that belonged to the Army since the days of the Spaniards—the Presidio. These fairgrounds bordered San Francisco Bay and extended from the city to the Golden Gate, where no one had yet been able to build a bridge.

Traveling to the fair on the western edge of the United States was an adventure in itself. Some people came by ship through the Panama Canal and were sorry. The Canal was still plagued by mud slides in some of its narrowest sections. At one time, 111 ships were lined up, waiting to go through as soon as the channel could be dredged again.

Most people went by train. "Club excursion" groups saved money by traveling together with their food and their babies packed in baskets. One old Idaho couple carried a bag of buffalo nickels they had saved to pay for their trip. Wealthy groups could hire a whole train—like the Billionaire's Express, which went up the coast from San Diego. Twelve coaches were fitted out like a fashionable house—with ballroom, orchestra, kitchen, lounges, and sleeping cars. The 125 guests were told they could take along everything they needed—so they took their manicurists, hairdressers, ladies' maids, stenographers, porters, bellboys, and doctors. By the time the Billionaire's Express arrived in San Francisco, few of the passengers could make it to the fairgrounds. They were exhausted from celebrating all the way there.

Millionaires owned their own private parlor cars, which were attached onto regularly scheduled express trains. They would have to rough it in 1915 because a new law forbade parking private railroad cars in the stations of large cities. They could still travel in their private Pullmans, but would have to make do with city hotel rooms while at the fair.

Hotels claimed they had not raised their prices. The Plaza and the Colonial cost $2 and up per person for a room with a private bath. The same room with meals cost $3.50 for one person and $6 for two. Another new law required that hotel beds be free from bedbugs and have sheets at least 98 inches long.

The most convenient hotel ($2 a day) was the Inside Inn, a temporary hotel inside the fairgrounds. The walls were so thin that people could get well acquainted with their neighbors without even meeting them.

The most adventurous way to go to the fair was to buy an automobile (a new one cost anywhere from $750 to $3,100 for a Packard) and drive there. The first road across the country would be the Lincoln Highway—if it ever got finished. During the rainy season, it was called the Lincoln Canal. From New York City to the Mississippi River, the roads were fairly good and easy to find. California roads were good and well-marked. But those few thousand miles in between were really bad.

Automobile touring required plenty of equipment—extra tires and inner tubes, water bags, tire chains, a block and tackle, inner tube patches and tire bandages, an electric bull's-eye lamp, rope, a compass and a road map, and dozens of emergency tools.

The biggest problems were broken springs and axles from hitting rocks and large holes in the road, and sand in the crankcase from fording muddy streams. But in spite of the hardships, travel by motorcar was increasing. An observer in one town on the unfinished Lincoln Highway counted 52 cars passing in June of 1913.

The newest art was aviation, in 1915. The tangled route of Art Smith's biplane shows one night's performance over the Tower of Jewels

But the year of the fair during the month of June, 225 cars passed his door!

No one in San Francisco could have slept later than 6:30 on the morning of February 20. Every noisemaker in the city was sounding off. Bells were ringing, horns were blowing, and sirens were shrieking for a full half hour. The citizens who had bought a badge that said "Participant" paraded through a special entrance gate into the fairgrounds. Sixteen marching bands kept the 150,000 laughing, singing people in stride.

The formal opening began later with an airplane circling the beautiful Tower of Jewels. Its pilot released six pure white doves as symbols of peace and prosperity. Upon receiving a telephone call at the White House in Washington, D.C., President Woodrow Wilson pushed a button to complete an electrical circuit over a telegraph line from the capital to a Navy radio telegraph station in Tuckerton, New Jersey. From there an 835-foot-high aerial relayed the message by radio to California, and the fair was officially ready to begin.

The telephone, telegraph, and radio were the newest, most exciting inventions of the age—or so the fair managers thought. They made wide aisles in the Electricity and Machinery buildings in anticipation of the huge crowds that would collect there. But the stars of this fair turned out to be automobiles, airplanes, and moving pictures.

As soon as they had paid their 50-cent admission fee, many people headed at once for the Palace of Transportation. There they crowded around the Ford Motor Assembly Plant to watch a 1915 Ford being built. First the front and rear axles and springs were attached to the frame. Then brake rods, fender irons, and gas tank were added. The motor, dashboard, and steering column were bolted in next. Each man along the assembly line had his job to do, and since he did it many times a day, he was assumed to be an expert at it. Finally the body of the Ford was mounted on the chassis, and the completed cars—25 of them every day—rolled off the end of the line. The lucky customer who had the cash (there were no charge cards then) could buy one, watch it being made, and drive it home. He could even buy for it the new "Gabriel Horn" which sounded four musical notes, "tee-poo-pee-pah," instead of "ooo-gah."

The airplane exhibit was disappointingly small. Several countries had kept their planes at home, since a war was threatening all of Europe. According to the newspapers, the French had a monster airplane that could carry a dozen armed men and fly up to 125 miles an hour. And the U.S. Navy had succeeded in launching an airplane from a battleship at sea—no one had invented the aircraft carrier yet.

Moving pictures were just getting started. D. W. Griffith's *The Clansman, or Birth of a Nation* was drawing record crowds at the Cort Theater in San Francisco. The film had the first battle scenes ever taken at night by a motion picture camera. The film's director had visited the Jewel City and was so impressed with it that he promised to use it as a background for his next movie. But he never did. A motion picture about the exposition, called *The Birth of the Jewel City,* was being shown in several large cities so people who could not reach the fair would be able to see it.

Movies, as a way of teaching, were very new. The pictures were only in black and white and there was no sound. When actors spoke lines that were important to the story, the words they spoke

Pale-pink palaces, turquoise arched ceilings, and a tower shimmering with 100,000 "jewels" thrilled visitors in San Francisco

were flashed onto the screen. Sometimes the words were obvious enough and did not have to be written out. Actors emoted a great deal, so that words would not be necessary—staring eyes and much deep breathing indicated great emotion, like love. The Jewel City had 73 motion picture theaters to show fairgoers everything from "how telegraph wires were strung across a mountain" to "life in the U.S. Navy" and "views of the Grand Canyon."

The exposition buildings were pale-pink palaces with red-tiled roofs. Because of San Francisco's wind, fog, sun, and rain, the buildings were grouped around small, cozy courts where flowers and plants thrived. The architecture, which had begun as a Far

Eastern style, ended with a little of everything from Greek, Roman, and French to Moorish, Gothic, and Spanish. All the arches and ceilings were deep blue. Ornaments and domes were deep gold and turquoise. On walls, flagpoles, and pennants there were touches of burnt orange beside the pink. Never had a fair been so colorful!

Set in the center was the unique Tower of Jewels. It loomed 45 stories above the main entrance and was covered with 100,000 "jewels" that had been made in Austria. Each of the "novagems," as they were called, was cut like a diamond and backed with a tiny mirror to make it reflect light and sparkle. They were of five colors —canary, amethyst, ruby, aquamarine, and white. The jewels were hung from the Tower on hooks so they could move in the wind, and sparkle. Admirers swiped so many from the top of the Tower the first two weeks of the fair that officials had to close it to sightseers.

In March, the fair managers thought a flock of pigeons would better dramatize the extreme height of the Tower's arches. Besides, just as people enjoyed feeding the famous pigeons at St. Mark's Square in Venice, they would enjoy feeding the birds here and having their pictures taken with them. Two thousand pigeons were invited to take up residence to "add a touch of life and color." By April, the people were starting to question the sanity of the man who had first thought of the pigeons. Didn't he know that 2,000 pigeons might have 2,000 friends, and that made 4,000 pigeons? No one knows how serious the pigeon menace might have become had it not been for the war in Europe. Thousands of the fair pigeons were volunteered to the Italian army and sent off in cages for messenger duty at the front.

Each of the Palaces had its chief attraction for the fairgoer. The Palace of Manufactures had a model home with everything electrical inside. Few people could believe that someday their own homes might have such wonders as electric refrigerators, electric suction cleaners to sweep their rugs, electric milk coolers and churns and butter makers, electric ranges to cook on, electric pumps to put out fires in their own homes, electric machines to do the laundry, wash the dishes, and even heat the baby's bottle.

In the Palace of Varied Industries were hand-knit sweater dresses from Argentina—suspected of being indecent because they clung so close to the body. At the Palace of Mines and Metallurgy, the crowds headed for a coal mine in a genuine vein of coal underneath the building. There they could also look through a telescope glass at a box that kept jiggling around because it had radium inside.

One of the most popular places to eat was the YWCA cafeteria. Cafeterias were such a new idea that society people were having "cafeteria parties" with silver trays and gourmet selections. One visitor, unused to the informal way Californians lived, was completely confused by the idea of a cafeteria line. She had to be led through it, and after finishing her lunch, she asked if now she was supposed to wash the dishes. By the time the fair closed, two new cafeterias had opened in San Francisco.

The time to visit the Palace of Food Products was lunchtime, when samples of food were handed out—Mexican tortillas, Southern corn bread, Russian rose cakes, French pastries, Swedish smobröd, and American flapjacks. With luck, a hungry visitor could visit the Heinz booth and sample a few of their 57 varieties which included euchred pickles, grapefruit marmalade, stuffed mangoes, pickled walnuts, and walnut catsup. The Jewel City was so famous for its scones—a flat biscuit served piping hot—that when San Francisco had its next fair twenty-four years later, the makers had to dig deep to find the original recipe they had served at the first fair.

At the Palace of Education, visiting teachers from all over the United States saw exciting new ways to teach children at home. There were giant Victrolas and the new ideas of Mme. Montessori, who taught a class of 21 children while visitors watched. But the most exciting new teaching tool was moving pictures. Some of the movies were even in color, but commercial color movies were still in the future.

Just before the fair opened, the first long-distance telephone call was made. Now a fairgoer could talk to any person who had a telephone and lived in any large city in the United States. Sometimes it took hours to complete a connection—from one operator to another through various cities between the two points—but eventually all the right wires were plugged into the right jacks and the caller could speak.

"And I could hear the voice very clearly!" was always the astonished reaction.

An even more thrilling event took place on September 29. The first transcontinental wireless telephony conversation took place between New York and California—today it's called "radio." Scientists were saying that someday people would even be able to talk to Europe without wires.

People were worried about the war that had begun in Europe. The idea of talking to Europe gave them the hope that wars might be avoided if only the leaders of countries about to go to war could talk with each other instead, at the moments of great tension. On May 8, Americans learned of the sinking of the *Lusitania* by a German torpedo. Even though the ship was British, the captain had often flown the American flag when sailing through dangerous waters, because America was still neutral. Now the *Lusitania* had been sunk with the loss of hundreds of lives—some of them American. The newspapers were filled with tragic stories from the survivors, but President Wilson seemed to be dillydallying about giving the Germans an ultimatum. Everyone hoped the new advances in communication would prevent any more disasters.

Fairgoers in 1915 were more or less bored with machines in the Machinery Building, like the one that made shoes and another that played the violin mechanically. The most unusual show was out back, where scientists had been secretly working all summer on a new electric machine to get rid of fog—something San Francisco had in great abundance. Sir Humphrey Davy had said that a small quantity of vapor was dissipated by a spark from a static machine, and this was the principle on which the Great Fog Machine was supposed to work.

The Fog Machine gave a great show. It could make 100-foot-long streaks of lightning, followed by terrifying thunderclaps. One day the giant transformer was linked to a wire screen placed twenty feet above the ground like the roof of a huge grape arbor. A crowd of curious people were allowed to walk beneath the electrical roof. They reported feeling such a strong electrical resistance that it was like walking in deep water. The machine was great for thrills, but useless for fog.

The Palace of Fine Arts was the one building that everyone planned to save after the Jewel City was gone. Since emphasis of the fair was on culture and the arts, and not on science and industry, the art collection was one of the finest ever seen in the United States. There was another reason, too. Most of the people of Europe now saw war threatening the borders of their own countries, and they reasoned that their finest works of art would be safer in a neutral country. Four million dollars' worth of Europe's greatest art arrived in the United States on an ugly coal ship that had dodged torpedoes and zeppelins all the way across the ocean.

As usual in the Palace of Fine Arts, there were complaints about the scanty clothing (or none at all) on the statues and the nude paintings. Leaders of the Ladies Purity League took time out from censoring the dancing ladies in the amusement area to claim that some of the statues were an insult to decency.

"How can a nude figure," they demanded, "possibly suggest winter?"

The artists answered, "Imagine representing the struggle of men and women seeking the goal of all earthly hope while dressed in fur overcoats, rubber boots, and overalls?"

The statue of the Pioneer Mother was much criticized because it was made by an Easterner (who presumably did not understand pioneer life) and because the children were undressed. (What pioneer mother would not cover her children?) The most-talked-about paintings were *September Morn* (a lady bathing in a lake) and *Stella*, who never made it to the Palace of Fine Arts because she was earning so much money down at the Joy Zone. Stella hid her nudity behind her arm, but she had a way of looking straight into the eyes of her beholders in a way that was shocking. Her best claim to fame was a good press agent. The advertisements— "Stella, Have You Seen Her?"—became part of American jargon for a few years.

One of the best-liked statues at the fair was James Earle Fraser's *End of the Trail*. It showed a dejected Indian sitting on his tired horse, obviously pushed to the very end of his trail by the white man. Fraser had wanted to see his statue on a point of land jutting out into the Pacific Ocean. Another of Fraser's works of art was the head of the Indian found on the buffalo nickel.

One of the cultural pursuits the fair emphasized was dancing. A famous dancer, La Loie Fuller, spent several weeks at the fair dancing dramatically with rainbows, soap bubbles, seashells, and yards of sunset-colored silks and chiffons wafting in the breeze. When she gave out, her place was taken by another dancer, Mlle. La Gai, who leaped about in the grass, followed by her barefoot child pupils all swathed in flowing chiffon. In their hands they carried wands so they could handle more yards of floating mate-

The statue of the dejected Indian and his horse who
have come to the end of their trail set people thinking in 1915

rial. The new free dance form was a deliberate attempt to get away from all the rules of ballet.

Social dancing, on the other hand, was about to change, according to the dancing masters of America. They were meeting at the fair to announce the death of such dances as the lame duck, the turkey trot, the fox-trot, and the kitchen sink. They pronounced the rag as vulgar. Naturally, that was the favorite of young people. Parents insisted that the rag was far too seductive for high school students, and teachers at Tamalpais High School claimed the best dancers of the rag had the worst report cards.

Young people were worrying their teachers and parents a great deal in 1915. Horrified parents discovered their daughters wearing transparent silk stockings, rubbing rouge on their cheeks, hiding lip pencils in their school kits, stuffing powder puffs into their shirts to add the bulges Nature had not yet supplied, wearing slit hobble skirts, and tucking switches and curls into their natural hair. A high school principal forbade boys to drive automobiles to school because "class snobbishness is promoted through the automobile habit."

While young girls often wore short sleeves and open-necked dresses, most ladies were clinging to long sleeves and skirts at least five feet wide at the hems. When one girl arrived at the exposition dressed in men's clothing (using the flimsy excuse that she thought men's clothes were more comfortable), she was turned away at the gates. An occasional woman dared to wear a "pants-skirt" and caused a considerable number of raised eyebrows. A man in New York was arrested for obstructing traffic because he wore a summer straw hat in February. Californians had voted against the sexless bathing suit for the beach. With a loose, blousy waist and a skirt below the knees, it was to be worn by both men and women. Instead, those who had nerve enough were buying the new one-piece knitted bathing suits that were displayed in the Palace of Varied Industries.

California women were freer than most. They had been voting since 1911. So when an airplane landed at the fairgrounds and Miss Catherine Stinson got out of the pilot's seat, no one was too surprised. When a bored young society girl, looking for new kicks, went up for a ride in the fair's sight-seeing plane, reporters were waiting to interview her when she landed.

"Oh, it was dandy," she gushed. "I liked it very much, but after all, it was not so much of a sensation as I had expected. I thought it would take the breath right out of me and scare me to death, but it didn't."

Taking people's breath and scaring them to death was the job of Lincoln Beachey, a young pilot who had been hired to provide thrills in the air three times a week. The one airplane on display at the Palace of Transportation was Beachey's biplane in which he made over 1,000 aerial loops. His feats were daring and sometimes crazy—like the day he decided to make the first "indoor flight" in the nave of the Machinery Building at the fair, before the machin-

Crowds headed for the yacht harbor to watch thrilling special events—like the airplane stunts, balloon races, and boat races

ery was moved in. He miscalculated the distance and ended up smashed against the wall at one end.

Every time Beachey flew at the Jewel City, he had a new death-defying stunt. In a memorable night flight, he climbed high in a series of spirals, tumbled over and over, then cut off his motor, turned earthward and plunged straight down—a long trail of blue vapor spewing out behind. The crowd was horrified. They could hear the wind making a loud hum through the wings of the plane as he suddenly pulled up just short of the ground. He had missed their hats by only a few feet!

Then one day in March, Beachey bought a new airplane—a monoplane. With 50,000 people watching, he tried the same trick. The wings of his new monoplane crumpled when he tried to straighten out.

"Oh, God! Beachey is gone," someone in the silent crowd shouted.

There was a rush for the edge of the marina as the plane plummeted straight down into the bay. For an hour the crowd stood watching while a diver from the battleship *Oregon* tried to locate the plane in the muddy bottom. Finally he managed to attach a wire around the tail, and the plane was winched up. Beachey was still strapped in the seat—uninjured, but drowned. In spite of his madcap tricks, Beachey had been trying to prove there was safety in flying. A few weeks before, he had written this:

"The next big battle of speed will be between airplanes. You do not have to worry about blowouts, mud, turns, or frictional accidents."

Beachey was referring to the dangers of racing in automobiles. The Jewel City had scheduled several auto races. One was the Grand Prix, with the course running through the fairgrounds. Out front for most of the race was Darius Resta. De Palma, a favorite to win, had quit when the race was half over because the road was too slippery to be safe. (There were no nonskid tires then.) Ten more drivers quit when it got dark. Then it was Hughes and Resta fighting it out in front. They disappeared around a curve and then only Resta was seen. What had happened to Hughes? Had he crashed at the turn? Had the fast clip proved fatal to his car? Suddenly his mechanic ran across the field to the pits.

"We are out of gas," he gasped, then raced back with three gallons. But it was too late. Resta had won, driving a Peugeot at an average speed (for over seven hours) of 56.1 miles an hour.

Fairgoers were not content with just racing cars or airplanes or boats. They had to pit the machines against each other. The Speed King's airplane and boat race was the result of a boast as to which was faster, speedboat or airplane. With 70,000 people watching, Wilbur J. Smith forced his motorboat *Oregon Kid* up to 45 miles an hour. In the air, Charles "Do Anything" Niles in his new Christofferson biplane, raced at 55 miles an hour. At one point, the birdman hovered playfully just above the speeding motorboat, then he gunned his motor and moved past, easily winning the race.

The Great Western Balloon Race was another special event. Four racers, each in his own balloon, were to race. Balloons were so unmanageable that the aeronauts who flew them could not be expected to land at a certain spot, so distance was the only way to measure a race. The takeoff was all the excitement any fairgoer could wish for.

Clarence Drake's *Queen of the Pacific* was swept over the marina and a large hole torn in the balloon before it was half filled with gas. Leon Brooks in the *Venice* barely had time to clamber into the basket when the same sudden gale wind caught his craft and dragged it along the ground.

"Turn her loose," he yelled to the ground crew trying to hold it down. "I'm going to make some sort of attempt anyway."

The basket bumped along the ground, dragging a few men who had not let go of the ropes quickly enough, rose 25 feet, then plopped into San Francisco Bay when the wind died just as suddenly as it had come up.

The only balloons that got away were George Harrison's *Jewel City* and Edward Unger's *California* (although it did not start until the next day). When they landed, officials still did not know who had won the race. One of the racers had landed farther from the starting point, but the other had actually traveled a longer distance. The judges finally gave the prize to Harrison.

A week later, Edward Unger set a new altitude record for balloons, reaching 28,900 feet. His landing that day was spectacular. He clipped several electric wires, putting nearby towns in darkness for the night. When the balloon finally hit the earth, Unger (still in the basket) looped the loop over the top of the balloon. Then he met real danger—in the person of a farmer with a pitchfork. He was held at bay until he paid $6 for the rows of beets he had just scraped up with his balloon.

Hundreds of important people visited the Jewel City to see its marvels. Helen Keller and her teacher, Mrs. Anne Sullivan Macy, were there on a speaking tour. Helen was especially fond of the educated horse on the Joy Zone. Billy Sunday, the fiery preacher, came and preached "acrobatically," removing his collar and coat. David R. Francis came, too. He had been president of the St. Louis fair in 1904 and had a message for San Franciscans.

"People told us there would be such a reaction after the 1904 closed," he said, "that we would be sorry we ever had it. But it's not true. St. Louis is better and San Francisco will be too for having it. There is an Exposition Philosophy that fairs serve more than anything else to educate the people, broaden their outlook, develop individualism, cement relations of different nations, and inspire the nation with patriotism."

It was for just that reason that Theodore Roosevelt had his say. Before he arrived, two pacifist speakers had been heard on the subject of the war in Europe and the sinking of the *Lusitania.* T. R. had another point of view.

"Damn the mollycoddles. I'm heartily sick of this wheedling, simpering, cry of peace at any price. . . . Saying nothing to offend any of those men over there is all very pretty, but what if they come from over there to offend us with those guns? . . . No good can come from telling a nation on the Fourth of July how great we are unless we are prepared to defend it the other 364 days."

Meanwhile, the afternoon and evening performances and the fireworks at night began to take on a more warlike look. Fake battleships were torpedoed, rockets were sent up as a signal to blow up mines in the bay, volleys of shots were fired from land batteries. One big event after the sinking of the *Lusitania* was the sinking of the old steamship *Amador,* which had been made to look like a battleship. It was a sight not soon to be forgotten, according to the local newspaper.

"Of a sudden, the scene of calm was disturbed by a terrific explosion. The crowd fell back. Then issued from the water a burst of smoke. A huge cloud of black . . . then fragments shot 200 feet high into the air. Water came in to the shore in a huge wave. Then the smoke was gone, and there was nothing left of the ship."

The crowd was satisfied now that they knew how the passengers on the *Lusitania* had felt. They wandered off to watch the "human elephant" walk a tightrope across the Joy Zone.

A young and reckless pilot named Art Smith was hired after Lincoln Beachey was killed. But Art Smith had orders not to take any chances. The crowd adored him. He flew several times a week and in between flights he kept his press agent busy advertising what feats of daring he would do for his next show.

Smith was famous for his imitation of a flaming comet, with fireworks shooting out the rear of his biplane. At night, he often did the "blind staggers" in which he rose from the ground enveloped in red fire. Then all was blackness until he reappeared wrapped in white fire. Suddenly there was only the darkness again, the purr of a faraway motor, and then, with a screaming roar, his plane would appear directly over the heads of the crowd in a burst of green fire.

No kind of weather kept Art Smith on the ground. He was as serious as Beachey about proving the safety of aircraft. He flew in fog that was so thick the watchers could hardly see the Tower of Jewels. And once when it hailed, Art came down with his face all red from being pelted with hail and said, "I was up there next to the faucet."

All of Art's antics were fuel for a crowd thirsty for thrills and hungry to have an idea of what the birdmen in Europe were doing on the battlefront.

Even though Europe was at war, most of the foreign pavilions at the fair were from the West and were open throughout the fair. China's contribution was a replica of one part of the Forbidden City of Peking. Fairgoers could walk where no outsider had ever set foot before—in the Imperial Audience Hall of Tai Wo. The walled city had gateways, pagodas, an ornamental tower, and some of the rarest works of art and silk paintings Americans have ever seen.

The Hawaii Building had an unusual aquarium filled with beautiful fish. An eminent doctor actually recommended that if nervous people had aquariums in their homes and would sit and watch the fish, their tensions would leave them at once. Thus began a new hobby.

*The Liberty Bell traveled from Philadelphia to San
Francisco in an open flatcar*

*Schoolchildren lined the tracks for a glimpse of the
bell*

*At the fair, the Liberty Bell was hoisted onto a float
for a parade*

Siam built an exact copy of a temple on the grounds of the Royal Palace at Bangkok for fair visitors to enjoy. Around the Australian Pavilion were kangaroos and wallabies. Australians were also selling calendars with a different view on each month's page. One lady who had heard that Australian time was a day ahead of U.S. time stopped to ask, "Are those calendars any good in this country?"

Many states had pavilions that were copies of famous historic buildings. Virginia had built Mt. Vernon, Tennessee had The Hermitage, Oregon had the Greek Parthenon, and Pennsylvania had Independence Hall.

The Liberty Bell was inside Pennsylvania's Independence Hall. This was the eighth and last time the old bell traveled to a world's fair. Philadelphians had complained about letting it leave the city —especially to travel all the way across the country. At first someone had suggested tapping the bell with a mallet and allowing the sound to travel over the long-distance telephone. But people wanted to see it and touch it.

The bell was finally loaded onto a flatcar, and a large committee traveled with it. One scientist said the bell was suffering from a rare metal disease and might fall into pieces before it arrived back home. So one of the committee had to measure the bell's crack every day to be sure it was not widening. But even the committee traveling with the bell were not prepared for the display of affection the bell received on its trip. Schoolchildren waited hours beside the track just to see the bell go by. In towns where the train stopped, special viewing platforms had been built so people could walk past to see it. Sometimes the travelers had glimpses of people standing alone to watch the train pass—an old hobo with his hat over his heart, a lonely family on a prairie so barren there was not even a tree, waving an American flag. At one little town along the way, a bouquet of flowers was tossed into the flatcar with this note attached:

Dear Old Liberty Bell,
   I haven't any money to go to the fair. So hope I will get a glimpse of you this morning. Good-bye. Hope you get home safe.

                              [Signed] Willie Jones of the
                              Whippoorwill Picket of Boy Scouts

Another of the thrills at the fair was watching the fire drills. Wooden shacks were burned in the North Gardens by the bay, and different companies competed in climbing ladders and shooting the lifeline up to the top of a high tower. Unfortunately, firemen failed to stop one tragic fire just outside the grounds in August, which killed a mother and her three little girls. The woman was the wife of General John J. Pershing, who had been called away to settle some military problems along the Mexican border. Only the general's little son, Warren, age five, was saved. In the near future, General Pershing was to lead American soldiers into war in Europe.

The Joy Zone was purely for fun. But a feature that showed there one week would not necessarily still be there the following week—thanks to the Purity League, which kept comparing the fun with the wicked Barbary Coast of San Francisco's clipper ship days.

One concession had been filled with people ever since the sinking of the *Lusitania* and rumors of German U-boats under the ocean. For 10 cents visitors took a trip in a make-believe submarine past fake sea monsters and shipwrecks. Others who wanted to understand the war filed into a concession called "The Evolution of the Dreadnaught," but found it contained more sailing ships than the dreadnaughts, larger than battleships. One day, fairgoers watched a sham battle between the *Monitor* and the *Merrimac* on the bay. The ships were fake, but the watchers had all the thrills of being in the battle. War was still so far away that Americans really believed the booms and flares of mortars and rockets gave an accurate picture of a battlefield.

The best show on the Joy Zone—and the one that every important visitor was taken to first—was the "Panama Canal." For 50 cents, a person had a bird's-eye view of the entire Canal Zone. He sat in a comfortable armchair with a pair of receivers over his ears so he could hear a description of the Zone as he circled it. The armchair rode about a third of a mile around a huge slowly moving platform showing a model that was claimed to be accurate down to the last tree and rock.

"The Dayton Flood" had only a different name to distinguish it from other floods at other fairs. The newspaper ad tried to make it sound new:

Not a Moving Picture

Real Water   Real Water

First time in any City—A Triumph of Ingenuity

The
DAYTON
FLOOD

The Scenic Production with a "Soul"

Neither Mythological nor Biblical—A Marvelous Reproduction
of a Great 20th Century Disaster!

Something Absolutely New   An Electrical Wonder

SEE   *The Rush of Mad Flood Waters*
The Great Snow Storm
The Flooded City of Fire
25 ¢   *The Beautiful Church Scene*   25 ¢

The baby incubators were not new either. The new feature in
1915 was that Dr. Couney, who was still traveling around with his
baby-saving invention, was now meeting some of the babies he
had saved. One infant was now a lovely young freshman at Vassar
College. Only nine years ago, Dr. Couney's own little girl had been
saved by the incubator. Now he was hoping to find someone who
would provide a building for his machines so he could stop traveling with expositions.

Alligators had appeared at fairs since the first one had been
shipped to New York in 1853 to be in one of the shacks outside the
Crystal Palace. Now Alligator Joe was enjoying a new fame in
California with his Florida reptiles and sea cows. The two states
were great rivals for the tourist trade, and Californians were only
too happy to have people see what monsters lived in "that other
state." They were even more delighted when Alligator Joe's animals died off so fast he had to close his concession early. It only
went to prove that such creatures could not exist in California's
healthy climate.

There were several foreign villages. The Tehuantepec Village
from Mexico had sunken water gardens filled with fragrant blossoms, and 20 "jungle queens" living there in thatched huts. A
Japanese village had Geisha dancers, top-spinning, jujitsu contests,
and Mount Fuji in miniature. But the strangest was Sid Grauman's

"Underground Chinatown" where the audience visited an opium den, a fan-tan parlor, and Chinese lottery games. As part of the fun, the audience was "pinched in a police raid." But the Chinese community of San Francisco had many respected businessmen who complained of this biased view of their Chinatown, and so the name was changed to "Underground Slumming."

"Toyland Grown Up" was a new concession idea based on the principle that adults are just kids grown tall. It was divided into Crazy Town, where everything was topsy-turvy; the Playground, which included a motorboat ride through a canal; and the Giant's Kitchen, where the furniture was the largest in the world. One of the unexpected sights here was a lady policeman. She was 6 feet 4 inches tall and weighed 200 pounds, a fact well advertised in case anyone planned to give her trouble. She was evidently having a hard time in those early days of women's liberation, because a poem appeared in the paper that began,

> Arrest me now, oh Fair Cop-ette.
> I'll go to jail with you.

Two of the exceptional shows on the Joy Zone were the "Grand Canyon" and "Yellowstone Park." They tried to give the visitors an accurate idea of what those two great national parks looked like. The visitor to the Grand Canyon sat in a parlor observation car and rode along the rim of a painted canvas canyon, looking out at seven of the most famous points. Yellowstone Park offered an inn with excellent meals, an 80-piece orchestra, and a Spectatorium where visitors could watch Old Faithful and other geysers by starlight and moonlight, at rosy dawn and at noontime.

The sight that people expected to remember most vividly fifty years after the Jewel City was gone was the way the fair looked at night. Earlier fairs had used gaslights to get a wavery effect. Others had electric lights that were almost blinding to eyes not used to bare electric bulbs. But in San Francisco, only indirect lighting was used.

Lights were hidden behind architecture and shrubbery. The walls of the Palaces were flooded by great arc lights hidden behind handsome brass shields. For the brightest lights ever seen by man, the bill came to $500 a night. There were 900 magnetite arc lamps, 347 searchlights, 250 incandescent projectors to light up

flags, 200 projectors of locomotive headlights to light up the statues, 250 high-pressure gas arc lamps for the streets of the state and
the foreign section, nearly 700 searchlight mirrors, and 30,000
incandescent bulbs—all hidden from view.

The "novagems" on the Tower of Jewels caught all the lights
and flashed them back. The glass dome of one palace was lighted
from inside by moving colored searchlights, giving it the effect of
a giant opal. But the most unusual light ever seen by anyone was
the Scintillator.

"Why bother with all those lights when half the time it will be
foggy anyway?" asked one of the early fair builders.

An engineer agreed that there must be some way to make use
of San Francisco's famous fog. He developed the Scintillator—a
lighting effect that made the Jewel City look like the home of the
northern lights.

The Scintillator sent out its colored rays so brightly from behind
the Tower of Jewels that scientists wondered whether earth people were attracting messages from another planet. That seemed
to be the only explanation for some weird and unexplainable lights
around the arches of the Tower. Blue and white flashes appeared
when the searchlights were pointed upward. Some of the wireless
equipment in the Palace of Liberal Arts misbehaved at the same
time. (Since the wireless was new to the people, static on it was also
new to them.) A direction detector seemed to be doing a violent
dance and pointing toward the top of the Tower of Jewels. Some
people thought the only answer was that beings on Mars were
trying to communicate with earth.

Although the Scintillator worked best in fog, there had to be
some way to make it work on fogless nights. A huge locomotive,
kept at the edge of the marina, was started up so it could chug up
clouds of steam to be lighted up by the northern lights effect.
Behind the locomotive were two huge standards with great
plumes of steam coming out, giving the effect of writhing snakes.
A pinwheel of steam between the engine and the audience made
it appear as if the locomotive were dashing full speed ahead. In
front of the pier was a realistic giant octopus—its arms reaching
up out of the water to grasp the engine.

Closing Day was both sad and hopeful. New discoveries were
already outdating some of the wonders that had thrilled audiences
when the fair opened. The U.S. Navy began to use airplanes to fly

overhead and warn their ships of submarines or enemy ships in their paths. If only the *Lusitania* had been protected by an airplane, people began to think sadly. A wireless operator in Honolulu had overheard a conversation taking place between Germany and Tuckerton, New Jersey—a distance of 9,000 miles! The war had worsened but the United States was still neutral, although some civilians had gone to army training camps during the summer for a few weeks' instruction.

On December 4, the city flags flew at half-mast to mark the passing of the incomparable Jewel City. Art Smith flew one last

Some people were afraid the bright lights of the Scintillator had attracted attention on Mars

time to write "Farewell" in the sky. A salvo of 635 bombs drowned out the bugler sounding taps and reminded people of the closeness of war. When the roar died down, lights on the Tower of Jewels spelled "Finis," everyone sang "Auld Lang Syne," and with "The Star-spangled Banner" the flag slowly descended. There was a momentary hush, then the crowd wandered away.

A few days later a different crowd was back—each person paying 25 cents to wander about the emptying Palaces, perhaps buy a few statues or pick up a memento, and watch the wreckers turn the fair into a sea of plaster dust. Buildings were sold to anyone who would buy—Norway's and Sweden's went for $150 and $500. The wreckers bought the $100,000 French Pavilion for $2,000.

The Siamese Pavilion was given to the city and was to be moved to Golden Gate Park. Since the Army owned most of the ground where the fair was built, some of the buildings were kept for a mess hall and an enlisted men's clubhouse. The Army decided also to keep the trotting park, drill ground, aviation field, athletic park, clubhouse, polo field, grandstands, and other buildings. A third of the U.S. Government exhibit was sent off to Panama, where the items could be seen at the Republic of Panama Exposition, which was to open on January 21, 1916.

Several works of art were bought by M. H. De Young and given to the city of San Francisco. Since the start of the fair, there had been plans to save the Palace of Fine Arts, but the city had very few art objects to put inside it. Eventually, the Palace was rebuilt at a cost of $10 million. It was still there the next time San Francisco had a big fair.

The statue of the Pioneer Mother was still there too, but it was moved to Treasure Island to hold a place of importance at the 1939 fair. The *End of the Trail* statue stood outside the Palace of the Legion of Honor for several years before it was moved to Visalia, California, where it stood at the entrance to Mooney Grove Park. In 1968, an author (Dean Krakel) was so interested in it that he wrote a book about it. He saw to it that a plaster mold was sent to Italy to be bronzed. The bronze version sits in the Hall of Fame on Persimmon Hill overlooking the Oklahoma capitol building. The original statue, plaster over chicken wire, went back to the park in Visalia, where it was bought by Dean Krakel and put in the Cowboy Hall of Fame.

The Tower of Jewels, which so many people tried to save, fell to the wrecker's ball. It was built of temporary materials and could not be saved.

Perhaps the most unusual after-exposition story is what happened to the Scintillator. Half of its super-projectors were bought for $24,000 by the Russian government in October (before the fair had ended) and sent immediately to the battlefield, where they were supposed to "turn night into day." As was true of so many human beings on the battlefields of World War I, the fate of the Scintillator is unknown.

World War I came and went, leaving people without the heart to have fairs for many years. Finally, in 1926, Philadelphia tried to have a sesquicentennial to celebrate the nation's 150th birthday, but the fair was a financial failure. What people remembered most about it was "the first electric house" with vacuum cleaner, washing machine, shortwave radio, and icebox—all run by electricity.

Everyone was feeling rich and the '20s were roaring when Long Beach, California, had its Pacific-Southwest Exposition in 1928. Sand dunes were changed into the Garden of Allah as a Tunisian village was created at the edge of the ocean. The most exciting features of this fair were watching an airplane being assembled and seeing the first talkies, a movie called *The Jazz Singer* with Al Jolson. This fair opened to a world of wealth and closed when the stock market crash created poor people almost overnight.

6
Chicago's "Rainbow City"
1933–1934

The new President, Franklin Delano Roosevelt, had just promised "a new deal" for everyone. Chrysler introduced the "Airflow" streamlined automobile, and the first streamlined high-speed train was about to appear on the rails, stopping at large cities across the United States to show people the meaning of the new word "streamlined."

Young people were doing the lindy to the music of swing bands, and everyone was humming Irving Berlin's "Easter Parade." At the movies, Ginger Rogers and Fred Astaire danced across the screen in *Flying Down to Rio*, while a little girl named Shirley Temple had just made her first movie. Thousands of people across the country were waiting hopefully for Chicago's exposition to open. The world was fairly peaceful, still unaware that one man in Germany had just reached a political position from which he would upset the entire world.

At first the fair was to be called the Chicago World's Fair Centennial Celebration because it was meant to celebrate that city's 100th birthday. Then when the fair managers decided to put the emphasis on science and its progress, the fair was renamed A Century of Progress. But as soon as it opened, the first fairgoers went home with a new name—"Rainbow City."

Rainbow City was built on an island that was not even there when Chicago had had its last fair in 1893. Northerly Island was made of pilings and filled-in land. The extra water was channeled into two large lakes called North and South Lagoons. The fair stretched for three miles along the shore of Lake Michigan, covering all the newly built island and the shore of the mainland.

"Vast numbers of people who knew nothing at all about any-

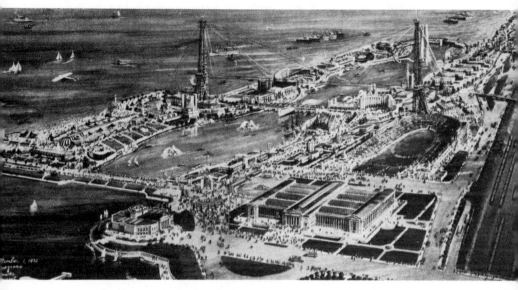

An island was built to hold Chicago's Century of Progress

thing in particular forty years ago know something imperfectly about everything now," complained one magazine when everyone had an idea of how the fair should be built. Some of the ideas were better filed in a wastebasket, like one suggestion of a building a thousand feet long in the shape of a giant pickle.

For the first time since 1893, the country's best architects were called together to help plan the Century of Progress. The chairman was Hubert Burnham, son of the man who had told 1893 fair architects to "make no little plans." This group also had pompous ideas—a great illuminated tower of celluloid, glass, and tile, taller than the Washington Monument, or a series of giant obelisks, or a cathedral-like building with fifteen aisles.

Shortly after the committee's first meeting, the stock market crashed. Millionaires became paupers overnight. A bitter depression followed, and most of the banks in the country closed their doors, so people in trouble were not even able to withdraw their savings.

The architects of the fair sat unhappily with their big ideas and empty pockets. They could not even afford a fair built in "art moderne." The buildings would have to be as plain as possible. And since it cost just as much to put windows in temporary buildings as in permanent ones, they could not even afford windows. Luckily there was now electricity for indoor lighting, and the first iced-air machines were capable of cooling during the summer heat. Instead of sculptured acanthus leaves, gargoyles, and Grecian maidens, the architects would have to settle for cold-water paint. At least they could afford color.

Some of the color combinations were startling—like pink, red, and violet all on one building. Or chartreuse and turquoise next to each other. Americans in 1933 were not yet used to color. Almost all their automobiles were black. An occasional bright-blue car with red wheels was seen only in auto shows and bought after the show by someone who could not afford the price of a new black car. All sinks and bathtubs came in white, except when an occasional wealthy person could afford to buy a tinted sink for a powder room. Even men's suits came only in black, brown, or dark blue. The Rainbow City featured color as never before.

One of the chief worries of the architects was what to set up as the super attraction—something like the Eiffel Tower erected in 1889 in Paris, the Ferris wheel in 1893, or the Tower of Jewels in 1915. Since the emphasis of the fair was to be on Science, the notion of rockets appealed strongly to the committee. No one knew much about rockets, except science fiction writers and Robert H. Goddard who had actually fired a rocket three years before which went 500 miles an hour. The suggestion was greeted with approval, anyway, and orders were sent out to build a "rocket ride" that would go across the water from the mainland to Northerly Island.

Plans for the opening had to be scientific, too. No telegraph key signals would do for the Century of Progress. What the scientists came up with was a fitting entry into the Space Age, although few people realized the world was on the threshold of that new era at the time. Astronomers pointed out that the light that had left one of the brightest stars in the sky, Arcturus, in 1893 when Chicago had its last fair, would be arriving here on earth in 1933.

With the help of the discovery of the photoelectric cell, which gives off slight voltage when a beam of light falls on it, the scientists captured the light from the star. The photoelectric cell was attached to the lower end of a telescope pointed toward Arcturus. An amplifier connected to the cell stepped up the slight electrical impulse. The impulses were sent from four observatories to the Hall of Science Court, where the total energy combined to throw a switch which turned on a searchlight on top of the carillon. That searchlight beam was then aimed at the electric eyes on top of the four principal fair buildings, thus making the fair suddenly blaze into light on June 1, 1933.

As soon as the fair lighted up, people could see there was a hot competition going between two kinds of lamps. The Century of Progress was to be a testing ground between the incandescent lights and a new kind of lighting in tubes. Rare gases sealed in the tubes gave off unusual effects when electric current activated them. Neon gases showed red, helium gases showed yellow, and

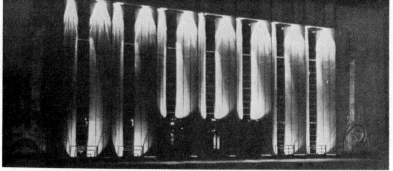

Lighting in tubes created unusual effects at night

krypton gas made blue light. Never had a fair or Midway been lighted so brilliantly.

Dazzling white shafts of light shone up the 64-story towers of the Sky Ride at night. The towers were higher than any building in downtown Chicago, and sightseers at the top could see four states. But the main purpose of the two towers was to support the rocketship ride. The rocketships traveled across cables at about the height of a 25-story building.

"Only the George Washington Bridge gives you a longer ride," said the advertising blurb. But the Sky Ride was sadly disappointing. Although the rockets carried 36 people and cost only 50 cents for a trip into the future, they whizzed across the cable at an agonizingly slow 5 miles an hour.

People arriving at the Century of Progress exposition were greeted by brilliant flashes of color. The Esplanade of Flags had hundreds of fluttering geranium-red banners. But flowers hardly

A rocket ship Sky Ride thrilled visitors with a vision of the Space Age that was coming

showed up against the sides of buildings painted all different colors. Admission to the fair was 50 cents for adults and 25 cents for children. Near the entrance were 10-cent Greyhound buses as well as rolling chairs and jinrickshas. The rolling chairs were pushed by football players, called "tea cart pushers" by the jinricksha men, who were all track men. They could have been the grandsons of the original pushers, who had had a similar feud going in 1893.

One of the most popular sights at the fair was the automobile exhibits. For the first time, new autos were not in the transportation building, but were shown by their manufacturers. Chrysler had a test track where viewers could stand on a balcony and watch cars go through their paces on a "torture track." To demonstrate the safety of the modern motorcar, a Graham-Paige car was driven 50 miles an hour through a wall. General Motors had the only building with glass walls for people to watch a car being assembled. A visitor could buy a Chevrolet in the morning, watch it being put together during the day, and drive it off the assembly line that evening. The Ford Motor Company ignored the fair in 1933, but the next year it put on an outdoor show called Roadways of the World.

Many drivers had come by auto to the fair, staying in cabins and tourist camps. There were no motels, only small separate cabins, each one costing from $1 to $5 a night no matter how many people were in it. The fair managers had asked state police to be "polite" to out-of-town drivers because there still were no standard rules throughout the states. But traffic jams were something new to Chicagoans. On the Fourth of July, they saw "the largest assembly of autos in the city's history." The parking lot which held 7,500 cars was suddenly flooded when over 18,500 autos appeared on the same day. Cars were parked everywhere imaginable—including all over the bus station parking lots, so the buses could not come or go.

A person could buy a Dodge 6 for $595 or a convertible coupé for $100 extra. Expensive tastes could be satisfied with a Pierce-Arrow 8 or 12 for about $2,500. But most young people bought used cars which had another ten years of life for less than $25.

The Gabriel Horn, which had made such a hit at the San Francisco 1915 fair, had a brief moment of fame in 1933 when the Nazis decreed that only Storm Troopers would be allowed to have the horn that went "tee-poo-pee-pah" on their cars in Germany. Few people who read that item in *Time* magazine really understood the menace that was beginning to grow in Germany during this first year the Nazi Party was in power. Gradually throughout the two years in which the Century of Progress celebrated advancement in science, stories of Nazi savagery began to collect.

The Nazis had insisted that Germany had only a small army of 100,000 men. They did not include in the count the 2,500,000 Storm Troopers. The brown uniform they wore, insisted their chief of staff, was completely unsuitable to wear in the field, so they could never be considered soldiers. Questioned about the last troop of German Boy Scouts who had just been turned into a Hitler Youth Group, the same man said he understood that all the youth of the United States were being trained now for war.

Actually, American Boy Scouts were serving as guides, message deliverers, and finders of missing children in the Rainbow City. They camped on the grounds of the exposition and were not allowed to take money for their services.

One way for people to find themselves who tended to get lost easily was to look for the huge Havoline thermometer that was 25 stories tall. It showed the temperature on its three sides with numerals 2 feet high. Some days people would have been happier not knowing how hot it was. Once when the red neon-tubing line hit 106°, the Chicago Symphony Orchestra stopped playing in the middle of a concert. In spite of the heat, no one wore shorts at the fair. Shorts were not even permitted at golf tournaments, even though one golf pro had said, "They are the only sensible thing to wear."

The Hall of Science was the largest building at the fair and stood out in yellow, orange, red, and white splendor. Orders were that science displays were to have no dull charts or dreary lectures. People especially enjoyed the X-ray exhibit. For the first time, they saw a full-length X-ray machine that could take a picture of the entire body. With smaller machines, a person could put his hand or foot behind the screen and look at his own bones. No one had any idea that such machines could be dangerous to anyone getting too much radiation.

In the Hall of Social Science, visitors could look at a sample city dump of 1893, a dump of 1933, and a section of a European cave that had been sealed in rock 50,000 years before. A Mayan temple from Yucatán, its walls covered with elaborate designs, attracted huge crowds. Harvard researchers in the Hall of Social Science interviewed over 3,000 fairgoers. They found that the average man there was 29 years old, 5 feet 8 inches tall, and weighed 153 pounds; the average woman was 31 years old, 5 feet 3 inches tall, and weighed 138.

In the Hall of Electricity, people could hear their own voices in different pitches and learn the mysteries of the dial telephone, soon to be installed in their own homes. Thomas Edison was the only man to have a memorial dedicated to him at the Rainbow City. Chicagoans had hoped to build the Hall of Electricity first of all, but had decided that many of its exhibits would be completely outdated by the time the fair opened, so fast were the changes coming.

Over 18 million Americans now had radio receiving sets, and so the Radio Palace was filled with people wondering what the new radios would be like. They were surprised to find that they wouldn't have larger, more handsome radios in their living rooms —the trend was toward making them smaller and more compact. Radio stars had become heroes. People listened to Eddie Cantor, George Burns and Gracie Allen, Jack Benny, and Ed Wynn for laughs. Rudy Vallee crooned soothingly, but a young man named Bing Crosby appealed more to younger people. Tears were shed daily over soap operas like *Just Plain Bill, Vic and Sade,* and *The Goldbergs.* Eno Crime Club and Charlie Chan had a wide variety of chilling sounds to make their mystery stories almost too real. At the Radio Palace, fairgoers learned for the first time how radio people made the sound effects during the stories that were broadcast every week—a miniature door with a handle and squeaky hinges sounded just like a full-size door when it was opened and shut, two blocks of wood with sandpaper on one side sounded like footsteps, and the rattling of a sheet of tin made convincing thunder.

Large groups of Polish children were taken to the Radio Palace to make records of their voices to send to grandparents in the Old World. For many of the grandparents, it would be the only word from their children in America before the Nazis invaded Poland. Poland's building at the fair was never occupied, so a group of German-Americans bought it and opened a restaurant.

Other European countries now began to feel the Nazis creeping closer. The people of Latvia woke one May morning to find their country under martial law and the Nazis in the streets of the capital. Hitler's advance men were spreading propaganda in Czechoslovakia, and the Czechs were so nervous that anyone who said "Heil Hitler" was arrested on the spot. In Germany, Storm Troopers shaved the head of a nineteen-year-old girl and dragged her through the streets of Nuremberg. She had dated a Jewish boy. A Nazi general was promoted when he ordered that no soldier could marry any girl with Jewish grandparents.

In Chicago, Jewish groups put on a spectacular show in Soldier Field called *Romance of a People.* The show was so popular that it had to be repeated for several days before audiences of all religions. Soldier Field was the scene of many sensational programs during the Century of Progress—from a science congress to the finals of the National Marbles Tournament. On special international days, dancing and performances by peoples of different nationalities were, for many, their last celebration because of the unrest in Europe. In July, the National Track and Field meet was held there, and for the first time in history, American athletes used the metric system for measurement in their events.

"A thumping spectacle" is what *Time* magazine called the Fourth Annual Chicagoland Music Festival in early September. In addition to the fireworks, young music lovers had "a nocturnal orgy of community singing and band playing" that drew 85,000 to the stadium. The music included Sousa marches (he hardly missed a fair!), popular tunes, and Tchaikovsky's "1812 Overture," complete with fireworks, cannons, and a 40-foot portrait in fireworks of Franklin Delano Roosevelt.

The world's fastest planes and flying aces went to the Gordon Bennett Balloon Race in September. There was intense competition in stunt flying, skywriting, autogiro flying, and parachute jumping contests. Air shows had been held all over the United States, and American pilots and planes were better for the experiences. Balloons, though, were not improving much. After a 7-hour ceremony that included bands, parades, an admiral and a general, "Tex" Settle took off on what was supposed to be the greatest balloon ascension ever made. Ten minutes later, Settle and his giant white rubberized balloon flopped down in the middle of the Chicago railroad yards.

In 1933, a passenger plane (express!) took 21 hours to fly from coast to coast. Quite a bit of that time was spent on the ground refueling and servicing the plane. But before the Rainbow City opened for its second year in 1934, a new type of airplane appeared. It crossed the country in an unbelievable 13 hours, traveling 220 miles an hour! Experts went wild with anticipation, predicting that someday airplanes might even reach 300 or 400 miles an hour. They might even travel in the stratosphere.

But there were accidents. Late one afternoon, Lake Michigan was squally and violent swells were building up along the shoreline. A group of passengers had paid for a ride in the sight-seeing seaplane.

"Do you think it's safe for landings?" an employee asked the pilot.

"I'll try just one more flight," he answered.

Seven or eight men and women climbed aboard for their tour. When the plane landed on the water, a wave broke the right pontoon. Quickly the pilot took off again for a landing field north of the city, but a mile before he reached it, the weakened right wing collapsed. The plane crashed and burned.

On July 4, the fair advertised that Uncle Sam would make a parachute jump from an airplane. After an extra-spectacular burst of rockets and with the band playing "The Star-spangled Banner," Uncle Sam tumbled out of the plane. The searchlights followed his drop, waiting for the chute to open. When he plummeted straight into the water, the crowd murmured, "A dummy, of course."

But Little Joe Wilson was not a dummy. His body was found the next day. To the horror of the man who had hired what he thought was a parachutist, Joe Wilson turned out to have been only an unemployed actor who had never jumped before in his life.

The Travel and Transport Building had a novel way of transporting visitors. In place of stairs, wheeled vehicles carried people up a ramp on an ultramodern escalator. Inside were displays of old-time autos, stagecoaches, prairie schooners, trains, and airplanes. But the best part of the show was a pageant called "Wings of a Century."

Fairgoers paid an extra 40 cents ($1 for a reserved seat) to see the show on a triple stage that included a railroad track and a highway, with Lake Michigan for a backdrop. The largest collection of historical vehicles ever seen at one time all took a part in the show. On the lake was the fastest ship of 1825, *The Baltimore*

Clipper. Famous old engines chugged and puffed along the stage track—including the DeWitt Clinton, which was getting to be a veteran fairgoer itself. On Opening Day of 1934, the diesel-powered Zephyr made a personal appearance on the stage. It had just broken all speed records for trains by traveling over 1,000 miles in 13 hours at an average of 77.6 miles an hour. Best of all, the Zephyr had used only $16 worth of crude oil for fuel. A steam locomotive would have used $225 worth of coal for the same trip. Perhaps the diesel locomotive would be able to bring the railroads back to the importance they once had.

World's fairs had a way of stimulating long lists of firsts. Some were good and others were silly. One first for Rainbow City was the Adler Planetarium which was inside the fairgrounds. It was the first planetarium in the United States. Another first was the dome on the Travel and Transport Building. Never before had architects built a dome so huge, held up by cables from the outside on the principle of a suspension bridge. Among the sillier firsts was the national egg-laying championship to be followed by the world's largest chicken fry. Another was the baseball players who wanted to try for a world's catching championship by catching a baseball thrown from the top of the Sky Ride Tower. The latter idea was finally canceled when someone who had studied mathematics in school calculated that the balls would be traveling at almost 137 miles an hour and, on the catchers' hands, they would hit like a 6,604-pound weight.

Children had a special exposition of their own at the "Enchanted Island." There they were greeted by a fairy princess, characters from storybooks, and a giant. Huge wooden soldiers, a straw man, the Tin Woodman, and a sailor whose arms revolved in the wind looked down from his 20-foot height. Children could explore a pirate's cave, a tree house, and a farmyard filled with baby animals. There was also a library and a children's theater with plays and puppet shows. They could ride a pony, a carousel, a zeppélin swing, or a drive-yourself auto. They could watch a miniature circus or educated monkeys. They could get lost in a

In a 1933 fair crowd, hardly a person could be found without a hat

CRANE

JOHNS-MANVILLE

US. STATION

WASTE
PAPER ONLY

23-2

privet hedge maze or go for a trip on a miniature railroad. Inside a Magic Mountain they found twisting caverns and a long slide down the hill.

Eating at the fair could be expensive or cheap. At the Century Grills, the fairgoer could buy a frankfurter and potato salad for 30 cents. A hot roast beef sandwich, pie or ice cream, coffee or milk cost 40 cents. Not a single hamburger was listed on the menu. Good eating could be had at any one of the foreign restaurants.

At the Victor Vienna Garden Café, the staff included a man who had cooked for the Emperor of Austria and the man who had managed "Old Vienna" at the 1893 fair. Everyone eating there realized that Austria was now under siege. They knew the streets of Vienna were filled with barbed wire and soldiers. On every border except the Hungarian, troops were massing. The Chancellor was given an ultimatum by the Nazis: accept a Nazi government in eight days or else . . . The Chancellor first took his family to safety in Italy, then returned to his country. He was murdered by the Nazis a few days later.

No great fair had been held since motion pictures had become the number one entertainment in the nation. Now visitors to Rainbow City could step right into Hollywood at the fair. They watched movies being filmed, saw radio shows being broadcast, had a peek at visiting celebrities, swam in the Malibu Pool (perhaps hoping some Hollywood director would wander nearby and spot them for a screen test), ate dinner in a copy of the famous Brown Derby restaurant (in the shape of a derby hat), and even shopped in some Hollywood type of stores where ladies could buy extreme movie star fashions.

Rainbow City visitors were especially eager to see the model homes. Everyone wanted to know what life would be like in the years to come. Prefabricated houses that could be assembled at the building site gave even the poorest person hopes of someday owning a home. Inside the model homes were dozens of tomorrow's gadgets. Some of the wonders promised in the next few years were pressure cookers, electric clothes dryers, new fly sprays (these later proved dangerous to man as well as to flies), washable wallpaper, unbreakable plastic dishes, colored sinks and bathtubs, metal awnings instead of canvas, a new metal called magnesium, a synthetic rubber with many possible uses, and for children, a safety lollipop with a looped handle instead of a dangerous wooden stick.

Also demonstrated was the possibility of transmitting pictures by radio—a hint of television to come. Some of the wonders faded away before they ever developed—like the colored enamel designs in milk bottles. Before too long, even milk bottles would disappear from the daily scene!

Model homes of another age could be found in a historic Lincoln Group, where five buildings associated with the famous man had been copied. The cabin in which he was born was actually built of logs taken from a house that had been standing for over a hundred years in Illinois. The clay for chinking between the logs had been brought from Kentucky. Visitors could wander through the Lincoln house of Little Pigeon Creek, Indiana, where Lincoln lived at the age of eight, and also through the general store from New Salem, Illinois. Hungry Lincoln fans could eat at the Rutledge Tavern, which featured steaks and chops broiled over charcoal and served "just as Lincoln might have been."

Historians had a harder time trying to rebuild Fort Dearborn exactly as it looked in 1812—the year it was destroyed and its inhabitants all killed by Indians. Only in Wisconsin could the builders find Norway pine to build the stockades and blockhouses and a straight slim spruce tree to use for the 70-foot flagpole. Stones that were the most weathered were chosen for the fireplaces. Glass that had flaws in it was selected for the windows. Inside, the furnishings had to be genuine old furniture—not just copies—for Chicago planned to keep the old fort for many years.

Chinese workmen came to Chicago especially to put together the 28,000-piece jigsaw puzzle that was the Golden Pavilion of Jehol, a Chinese Lama Temple where the Manchu emperors had worshiped until the revolution in 1911. With workmanship almost unbelievable to western hemisphere builders, the pieces were cut, carved, and fit together without a single nail. Over a million people paid to see the temple with its red lacquered columns and roof covered with 23-carat gold leaf. Gilded images of dragons, cats, and dogs covered the cornice beams. Inside, bronze and gold Buddhas, incense burners, trumpets, masks used in sacred dances, silver lamps, temple bells, and rare tapestries spirited fair visitors far away from Chicago.

Below the level of Lake Michigan was a tunnel down to the South African Diamond Mine. There, fairgoers watched Kaffir and Zulu laborers drilling and digging in the "blue ground." Two real diamond mine engineers were in charge of the diggings. They were also to make certain that no one ran off with the 3,000-carat supply of genuine "raw" diamonds that had been shipped from Kimberley to be "discovered" and dug out of the mine while spectators watched.

The Midway was purely for fun at this fair. Many of its shows were the same old standbys that had pleased other generations at other fairs. The giant paintings of war in Gettysburg and during World War I were still attracting the curious. So were alligator wrestlers, roller coasters, freaks of all sizes and shapes, reptiles, and the Midget Village. The incubator babies had larger crowds than ever because of the birth of the Dionne quintuplets during the second year of the fair—all five babies were kept alive in incubators.

A few new ideas appeared on the Rainbow City Midway. A two-deck Dance Ship, boasting two dance floors and orchestras, cruised along the lakeshore every evening. The Thrill House of Crime reminded ghoulish audiences of the recent Lindbergh baby kidnapping and of mobsters like Capone, Dillinger, and "Baby-face" Nelson. Egypt had lost none of its strange attraction for fair crowds through the years. This time it was a concession called Temple of Mystery. Carter the Great offered pictures showing how Howard Carter, the Egyptologist, had opened the tomb of Tutankhamen, the boy king of Egypt whose popularity has continued through the years.

The World a Million Years Ago bent historical accuracy badly in order to show people how it was to live in the age of dinosaurs— even though human beings never shared the planet with them. Visitors who parted with their money for this concession saw a caveman and cavewoman crouching in their cave while, outside, mechanical sabre-toothed tigers, mammoths, dinosaurs, and woolly rhinos stomped and roared, turning their heads and lashing their tails in pretend fury.

The usual foreign villages opened their cash registers to take in customers who wanted a view of ancient Egypt, the Ukraine, Morocco, Seminole Indians, Damascus, Tunis, Tripoli, Algiers, and Cairo. There was none of the seriousness about making the villages perfect as there had been in 1893. Old Belgium, with its Flemish houses and dogs pulling milk carts through the streets, was the best of the villages, while the Black Forest Village brought in the

Mechanical dinosaurs were popular with all ages

most money because it had an open-air ice-skating rink.

One of the most publicized villages began almost by accident. A group of people, trying to make money for the Century of Progress before the fair opened, had a party with a Streets of Paris theme. A lady dressed only in a long blond wig was hired to ride through the "streets" on a white horse. The party was such a success that the Streets of Paris was signed up to appear on the Midway. The lady, who turned out to be a fan dancer named Sally Rand, was hired, too. Sally Rand soon made oldsters forget about the educated muscles of "Little Egypt" they had admired back in 1893.

The Century of Progress was supposed to close on October 31, 1933. For another cold twelve days in November it was held open, but by then the managers had decided to hold the fair over for another year. They were still $4 million in debt and they hoped that with another year to attract crowds the fair could break even. New concessions and exhibits, cheaper buses, and new lighting effects should bring more people.

At long last, the Rainbow City came to its closing day on October 31, 1934. The wreckers arrived in December. Many exhibits went to the Chicago Museum of Science and Industry—itself a reconstruction in limestone and marble of the old 1893 Fine Arts Building. Some of the special buildings and exhibits were stored away, since only five years later large fairs were to be held in both New York and San Francisco.

The Adler Planetarium, which was not built just for the fair, remained on Northerly Island, and so did the bridges and ap-

Cobblestone streets and dogcarts made the Belgian Village seem real

proaches to it. The salvage company set up a yard and sold every-thing from pieces of steel to lightbulbs. A candy company bought part of the Agricultural Building to enlarge its factory. Model houses were loaded onto barges and many were towed to sites (and new owners) on the Indiana dunes east of Chicago.

The Chinese Lama Temple was left to stand until the gold-leaf paint on the roof began peeling off. Then it was packed away in a warehouse in 1937 and borrowed for the New York Fair in 1939.

Fort Dearborn remained, but, like the original fort, it was also burned down by savages (vandals this time) during the summer of 1940. The Administration Building became the Park Board Building.

Taking down the Sky Ride was the hardest job. Its builders had said, "The Sky Ride will live forever as a monument to a new principle." They were overconfident. Thermite fires were built around two legs of each tower. Quickly the two monsters buckled and collapsed. Something about the sight turned the watching crowd into a mob. They went through the fairgrounds taking every movable object they could find—trees, shrubs, floodlights, benches, stools, doors, and signs. The grounds were picked clean.

Like most fairs, the Century of Progress was not a complete financial success. Its success had to be measured in other ways. The emphasis on science had brought about improvements in communication and transportation that were vital to the United States, for war was to come only a few more years in the future. Before the next world's fair opened five years later, America had sulfa drugs, FM radio broadcasting, intravenous anesthesia, improved helicopters, radar detection, the ability to land airplanes in fog by the use of a radio beam, nylon, fiberglass, and diesel-motored trains—all thanks to the progress in the Rainbow City.

In the next few years, each corner of the country had its fair. The California Pacific Exposition drew crowds and businesses toward San Diego on the West Coast in 1935. The Texas Centennial in 1936 attracted fairgoers to Dallas. There was the World of the Great Lakes Exposition in Cleveland the same year. But news from Europe was more ominous as time for the great fairs of New York City and San Francisco drew near. Some people even wondered whether the big events to be held in 1939 would have to be canceled.

7

San Francisco's "Treasure Island" and New York's "World of Tomorrow" 1939–1940

Most teen-agers in the United States in 1939 did not dream that a war was coming and that they would soon be serving on the battlefields of Europe and Asia. For years the newspapers had carried stories of terrible things happening to the Jewish people and to people of small countries that had been invaded by the Nazis. But young people on this side of the ocean had no way of knowing that a war elsewhere in the world would inevitably affect their own country.

Young people that year were more concerned with what was showing at the local movie house on Saturday; the unfairness of Marian Anderson's not being allowed to sing in two Washington, D.C., auditoriums because she was black; the picnic lunch of hot dogs that President Franklin D. Roosevelt fed to the King and Queen of England; and the two fairs that were to be held on opposite coasts of the United States.

San Francisco's fair was in honor of its two new bridges. The Golden Gate Bridge had been built across a narrow inlet where the Pacific Ocean poured its waters swiftly and dangerously into San Francisco Bay. The Oakland Bay Bridge had been built across the huge bay to join two large cities. Because the distance was so great, the bridge stopped on Yerba Buena Island in the middle of the bay before continuing its journey. The northern end of Yerba Buena had long been a hazard to shipping because of its shoals. So while the bridge was built, the shoals were outlined with a wall of piers, and the land was filled in to form a new island—called Treasure Island. That was the site of the new fair.

New York City's fair, its first since the Crystal Palace, was to celebrate the inauguration of President George Washington in

The China Clipper *flies over the Golden Gate Bridge shortly after the first cables are stretched across the water. In the distance, the Oakland Bay Bridge reaches out toward Treasure Island, where the fair was to be held in 1939*

that city 150 years before. New York had little open space for building a fair—but there was the Corona Dumps—a swampy area in Queens that emptied its waters into Flushing Bay. It had been a garbage dump for years and boasted a 100-foot-high ash pile called Mount Corona. Before the garbage was piled there, the swamp's single claim to fame had been that George Washington crossed it in 1790 on his way to Flushing Bay. Turning that area into a park was to be the largest reclamation project in the Eastern States.

Waiting for the fairs to be built, American teen-agers had a little more time to be young than European young people. They had the largest selection of good movies that ever came from Holly-wood—*The Wizard of Oz, Snow White and the Seven Dwarfs, Stagecoach,* and soon they would be seeing *Gone with the Wind.* John Steinbeck's *Grapes of Wrath* was the best-known book, and the year before, Pearl Buck's *The Good Earth* had won a Nobel Prize. Paperback versions of good books (called "pocket books") could be bought for 25 cents and 35 cents. Irving Berlin's "God Bless America" was sweeping the country, but the young people were jitterbugging, shagging, and trucking to the tunes of great name bands. The most unusual radio program ever aired had terrified listeners into believing the world had really been invaded by Martians—when Orson Welles's program *The War of the Worlds* had come over the airwaves a little too realistically. The Sunday newspapers all had large sections of comics in color—*Joe Palooka* (a peaceful prizefighter), *Terry and the Pirates* (adventures in the Far East), *Tailspin Tommy* (an aviator), and assorted detectives, Indians, working girls, and science fiction stories.

Girls wore their hair as much like Scarlett O'Hara as possible. Their dresses and coats had wide padded shoulders that made any size waist look small by comparison. Skirts were well below the knee, and one-piece playsuits had wraparound skirts to wear to and from the tennis court. Boys wore corduroy trousers—only farmers wore dungarees. Everyone wore hats. Stockings were made of silk (very expensive and not long-wearing) or cheaper rayon. Rayon stockings bagged as soon as a girl sat down, and the knees of the stockings never did pull tight again. They had seams down the back that resisted all attempts to keep them straight.

On a cold and foggy day, California's Golden Gate International Exposition (known as "Treasure Island") opened—it was Friday, February 17, 1939. For a week before, San Franciscans had been celebrating with fireworks, beauty contests, parades, costume balls, and street dancing. Everyone dressed "Western style" and joined merrily in the 30-second noise periods three times a day all week. Sirens screamed, steamboats whistled, and factory whistles blared along with citizens' noisemakers.

The official ceremony, as befitted a Space Age fair, was as complicated as scientists could make it. Opening time was set for 10:30 P.M. because it would then be high noon in Bombay, India. A photoelectric cell in Bombay trapped power from the sun's rays and flashed it 9,000 miles by radio to the Tower of the Sun. The

The fair opened at night with a blaze of unusual lighting effects

*"Baghdad on the Bay" was on a man-made island in
San Francisco Bay*

Tower's 44-bell carillon began to play. President Franklin D. Roosevelt broadcast a speech for the opening from a warship in the Caribbean on the other side of the world from Bombay. Immediately the Scintillator blazed forth with over a billion candlepower. Black light, a weird new discovery, created strange effects. Just to make sure the fair opening was not lacking in grandeur, the fair officials used a huge golden key, which cost $35,000, to open the main gates.

Visitors poured through the entrances, paying 50 cents each. Some had driven across the new Oakland Bay Bridge to park on the island. Some just drove across the bridge in the hope of seeing the fair as they passed over it. But the bridge engineers had designed the guardrail so that automobile passengers could see nothing at all through the railing unless the car was traveling between 35 and 50 miles an hour. Some fair visitors took the 10-cent ferry over from San Francisco. Others came by train. The railroads offered a round trip to both fairs for $90—"8,000 miles for 9,000 pennies." A few of the visitors came by airplane. Flying was still so new that most people did not trust planes. Airports were very small buildings, and the passenger simply walked through a gate in a fence, climbed some steps to the plane, and took his seat with about 20 or 30 other passengers.

The *China Clipper* was the real star of the Golden Gate International. It was the largest flying boat in the world. Treasure Island had really been built especially to become the airport for the huge seaplanes after the fair ended. During the fair, thousands of people crowded into the Pan American mini-airport to watch the planes being serviced for their next trips. No plane ever took off for the Far East without a flock of people watching. But soon there were larger airplanes—the 74-passenger Boeing *Clipper* which had three motors. And in the Federal Building was shown an even larger plane, called the *Flying Fortress,* which would soon play a very important part in the war.

"It's Baghdad on the Bay!" shouted the newspaper headlines the first day the fair opened. The buildings had been made of stucco, with a micalike substance called vermiculite (used now for insulation) that was put on when the stucco was wet. The walls glittered a little as had the Tower of Jewels in 1915. Treasure Island had a huge Tower of the Sun, flanked by the Elephant Gates like two Mayan temples with stylized elephants on top. Presiding over a courtyard and facing the Tower of the Sun was a monster statue of *Pacifica,* who represented all the nations around the Pacific Ocean appearing at the fair. Behind *Pacifica* was a great metal curtain spangled with stars that were supposed to blow and tinkle in the breeze. When they did not, an architect attached a motor to push them back and forth until they clanged like camel bells.

The Big Bertha searchlights and the Scintillator could be seen fifty miles out at sea. The fountains looked like liquid gold when they were lighted at night. All the colors at the fair had been selected by a psychologist, who used them as a painter uses paints. The streetlights, designed to look like Siamese court parasols, were a warm amber color which the psychologist said would make people feel cool on warm nights and warm when it was cold. Shades of red and orange were used to excite people toward gaiety along the fun zone. Green and blue lights were placed where the psychologist wanted people to turn to a more reflective mood. Fluorescent paint produced a strange effect under black lighting at night, but this was not the choice of the color psychologist.

The purpose of Treasure Island was to promote understanding between the eleven states farthest west and the countries that lined the Pacific basin. There were a few hidden purposes, too. The fair was going to help pay for a new airport at Treasure Island. It also served the purpose of cheering people during hard times, although it did not succeed in promoting peace—even with the Pacific nations.

Flowers and trees were barged across the bay from the mainland to brighten the man-made island. In front of the main entrance was a dazzling Magic Carpet of ice plants that looked like a tremendous Oriental rug.

Treasure Island was filled with wonders, and as usual they were not always the ones the fair managers had expected to take the public eye. One of the marvels was a nylon stocking at the Dupont exhibit—an artificial hand stretching it over and over for weeks. Women demanded to know how soon the new kind of stocking would be for sale in the stores, and the company promised them by 1940. (Women had only a very short time to enjoy nylon stockings, because the company shortly began to make war materials instead.) Other wonders were the FM radio and the shortwave radio. People had "shortwave parties," with all the guests listening to voices from Europe. Businessmen were interested in seeing the electric typewriter which was so sensitive the keys could be worked with the touch of a feather—this later proved not so handy when a stenographer sneezed and set off a whole line of typewritten gobbledygook.

The greatest wonder of all was radioed pictures. There were only five "video" sets in the entire bay area, and they were all at the fair. The only picture programs broadcast also took place at the fair. But the wireless electronic picture looked like a great invention. For years, people had expected telephones that showed the person being spoken to, but "television" was even more promising. In 1940, for the first time, people saw the presidential election returns, as Franklin Delano Roosevelt won over the Republican, Wendell Willkie.

In the Hall of Electricity were kitchens of the future, robots that could talk and walk, toy electric trains that were controlled by voice, and a "magic bowl" that used repellent magnets to hold it suspended in midair. The Hall of Science had an atom-smashing cyclotron that would make possible the synthetic production of radioactive materials. The possibility of an atom bomb had been mentioned once by Albert Einstein in 1934, but very few people had any idea what a monster the atom smasher was capable of creating. Many medical advances were shown—certain types of pneumonia could now be controlled, insulin was giving new hope to diabetics, and there were many improvements in plastic surgery (tragically, soon to be needed for wartime injuries).

America! Cavalcade of a Nation was a rather Hollywoodized version of the settling of the West performed three times a day. The stage and arena filled eight acres and included mountains and railroad tracks. There was a finale with 48 horsemen dashing across the stage carrying the flags of the states and 4 carrying American flags. It was a time for patriotic shows, and this one always had a full house.

For the first time, industries had large displays at U.S. fairs. The U.S. Steel Company showed "the San Francisco of the future," with landscaped walkways for people, streets overhead, and office buildings designed to let the light in. They guessed wrong, however, when they added a giant pier filled with ocean liners from all over the world. The day of the ocean liner was already coming to an end.

Almost every star of stage or screen visited Treasure Island. One was Eddie Cantor, loved for his big silly grin and popeyes. In his serious moments, Cantor had successfully found homes in America for over 1,500 child refugees from Europe. One day he was asked to open the new Civic Auditorium. He yanked a lever, as the master of ceremonies had told him to do, and a faint whistling noise was heard. Then smoke poured out. Cantor's famous bug-eyes bugged out even farther as the whistle rose to a scream. He skipped aside quickly as the box exploded harmlessly. Someone had slipped a trick bomb into the box as a joke.

"Whew," said Cantor, "I thought Hitler was going to pop out."

Hitler was anything but idle during the early days of the fair. Periodically, the newspaper reported him dead and inserted hopeful headlines such as "Herr Hitler Riding for a Fall" and "Mussolini's Speech Today May Ease Tension." Meanwhile, the Czechoslovakian pavilion never opened. The Italian pavilion had a model of the next world's fair that was planned for Rome in 1942. Foreign pavilions tried to hang on through 1939, but most had packed up and gone home by the end of October, even though the fair managers had decided Treasure Island would be given another year to live.

The fun zone of the Golden Gate International was called the Gayway. Even in 1939, amusement area committees were still thinking in terms of the shantytown concessions of past fairs. Treasure Island had its roller coasters. It had a 30-foot python named Elmer, who came with ten beautiful girl handlers. It had a booth with the "deadliest snakes in the world," and the incubator babies. (The first babies would by now be fifty years old!)

The merchants of San Francisco's Chinatown built a beautiful Chinese village on the Gayway costing over $2 million. They wanted to make sure there was no repeat performance of the ugly "Underground Chinatown" concession of the 1915 fair. The new village included a huge red-and-gold pagoda, lacquerware sold at the Foochow Bazaar, and a fortune-teller who had a lark that selected each person's fortune. Chinese girls sang and played on butterfly harps and moon viols, while visitors ate Peking wind-blown duck at the Wing Restaurant.

Cheaper meals could be found at the Jolly Roger restaurants, where the food came out of the kitchen on a rubber belt. The waitress, selected for her pleasing voice, was forbidden to yell orders to the cook. A "Jolly Roger Treasure Island Imperial Hamburger" cost 20 cents and a T-bone steak was a dollar. Waitresses were paid very little, and customers were not very generous with tips. One waitress, though, did get a 50-cent tip—after she saw that a customer had forgotten her purse (with $2,000 inside) and ran out to find her.

Another group not getting enough pay were the chair-pushing boys. They averaged about $2 a day for wheeling around foot-weary visitors and answering their silly questions.

"When do they feed the lagoon?" asked one.

"Are they going to tear down the bridges, too, when the fair ends?" asked another. Some people just stopped the chair boys and asked dazedly, "Where do I want to go?"

On Easter Sunday, Marian Anderson sang to an audience of 75,000 from the steps of the Lincoln Memorial in Washington, D.C. The Dutch were mustering an army and sending the soldiers to the borders. Mussolini's army had invaded Albania. Hitler's Nazis were taking over Lithuania, while Hitler announced he was mapping a "World Peace Plan" of his own. Poland was arming its border and saying, "We won't yield an inch." At Treasure Island, one of Poland's most beloved pianists, Ignace Jan Paderewski, gave one of his finest concerts.

The Golden Gate International was not making money. In fact, it was close to "broke" by the end of April when the New York fair opened. Perhaps the managers' biggest mistake was opening in February when the weather across most of the nation was not the kind that makes people want to go to fairs. It was the schoolchildren who saved Treasure Island. Someone decided that the children should be sent to the fair by the busload for 10 cents per child. Thousands of children went and then returned during the summer, dragging two parents each.

Treasure Island was a today fair, with only a few glances back into the past. But New York's World of Tomorrow was the first fair in history ever to focus entirely on the future. For months before the opening, the slogan "Dawn of a New Day" had been the theme of parties and money-raising celebrations. Electric signs flashed Dawn of a New Day messages while bands played Gershwin's song of the same name. The "Coronation Scot," a streamlined train, toured 37 cities across the United States, with one car devoted to advertising the World of Tomorrow.

The World of Tomorrow opened on April 30 with the usual

*Crowds gathered to watch the World of Tomorrow
being built*

science fiction tricks of capturing cosmic rays with a photoelectric
cell to flick on a master switch. The New York fair was three times
the size of Chicago's in 1933. The theme "Building the World of
Tomorrow" was hard on architects who had to use the materials
of today. They solved that by designing buildings that looked as if
they had come from another planet—windowless, one-storied,
and streamlined.

Color had become very important to fairs. The World of Tomorrow was color-coded. Only the Trylon and Perisphere (symbols of
the future world) were pure white. Buildings closest to them were
very pale shades, gradually growing darker in color toward the

outside edges of the fair. From the air, the exposition must have looked like an artist's giant color wheel. Visitors who tended to get lost easily could just choose a color, keep walking until it got paler, and reach the center of the grounds. Everywhere orange and blue flags fluttered, and public buildings were identified by orange and blue. America was growing to love color in automobiles and homes. Now the model city of the fair was trying to suggest that more color would not hurt American cities either.

The Trylon, a three-sided figure as high as a 65-story building, symbolized the fair's lofty purpose. It had nothing inside, but merely served as the entrance to the great circular ramp that led into the Perisphere. This was a huge hollow globe, 18 stories high, which looked from a distance as if it were floating on top of bubbling fountains of water. Visitors ascended two of the longest moving stairways ever seen and entered the Perisphere to get a view of "Democracity." Two balconies, revolving in opposite directions, carried unending lines of people completely around the model city.

Democracity had wide highways and electrified trains to carry office workers into the city. Citizens all lived in gardenlike apartments outside the city. Factories had been banished to satellite towns so that their fumes and smoke would not annoy people (there was no thought then of the damage factories could be doing to nature). The viewers saw the city by day and night, with a hidden chorus of marching workingmen singing a rousing working song.

Some people thought a more realistic view of the future could be found in the Transportation Exhibit. There a movie showed an imaginary rocket ship flight from New York to London "via the stratosphere." In the movie, the passengers entered the rocket ship. Then a giant crane with a magnet on the end lifted the ship and deposited it into the barrel of a rocket gun. There was a momentary silence. Then a bright flash . . . a muffled explosion . . . and the ship vanished into the beyond. The movie had no suggestion of launching rockets, rocket engines, or even a suggestion of an orbit.

Twenty-five million people got their ideas of the future from the General Motors Futurama which predicted what the world would be like in 1960. The people sat in comfortable chairs that had loudspeakers concealed in the upholstery and rode through the

The star of the fair was television—seen on tiny screens while people waited in lines for a chance to look

largest animated scale model in the world. They saw interstate superhighways with a 100 mile an hour speed limit and expressways that carved right through cities. In 1939, a superhighway was one that had two lanes of traffic in each direction—and there were not many roads that large. As for expressways, the only way then to get through a city was to follow the route signs that took the unhappy motorist straight through the busiest section. Futurama had an unusual way for cars to enter the superhighways, a spiral ramp which looked like a cloverleaf. Skyscrapers were 150 stories high, and people in the city had walkways to keep them far from automobile traffic. But what shocked Futurama visitors the most was the prediction that by 1960 there would be 38 million cars on the roads. Actually, the number would come to almost double that figure.

Predicting what life would be like in the future was always risky. There were already enough wonders to gape at. Du Pont showed nylon material—before long it would prove indispensable to parachutists. (After the war, many brides made their wedding dresses of the parachute material.) Crossley had built an economy car, but it looked too small next to the other cars, which were growing larger every year. The Crossley designer was ahead of his time—there were no worries about gasoline shortages yet. Little girls found that the new soft plastics had advantages—they could now have dolls like Dy Dee doll and Betsy-Wetsy that were more like real babies. The vivid colors of Kodachrome slides were exciting to many, especially since color photographs taken with ordinary box cameras had such dull colors and tended to fade if left in the daylight. Radio had a new touch that people thought might be fine at the movies, but certainly not in the home—stereophonic sound.

Television was the most exciting new discovery of all. Although only a handful of people had a television set and there were no regular broadcasts, the fair exhibits made it plain that soon the sets would be available to anyone who could afford to pay about $700. The new machine had a mirror that reflected the picture shown on the horizontal tube so the viewer could see it sitting down in a room. Crowds packed around the tiny screens to see the miracle.

Westinghouse scientists buried a time capsule which was to be opened five thousand years after the fair. To make sure the capsule could be found in fifty centuries, they made it of the sturdiest metal available—a copper alloy called Cupaloy. Scientists felt that archaeologists in A.D 6939 would be able to reconstruct the dams, roads, and houses, but that some of the everyday life of 1939 might otherwise be lost forever.

The capsule holds books and photographs to show how Americans lived and worked, their machines, arts, entertainments, newspapers, magazines, and even comics. Copies of the Bible and the U.S. Constitution are there, along with astronomical observations (in 1939, there were two eclipses of the moon and two of the sun) and history books. There are ideas of clothing (including a woman's hat), farm products, medicines, eyeglasses, cosmetics, the Lord's Prayer in 300 languages, a fable "The North Wind and the Sun" (a story that is common to many countries), and a key for pronouncing the English language. Only the Bible and the book explaining how and why the capsule was buried are in normal size —the others are on microfilm.

The World of Tomorrow had its artists. Alexander Calder's water ballet appeared for the first time to thrill audiences with the beauties of color and changing fountains with a musical background. There has hardly been a great American fair without an artist named Calder. Alexander's grandfather, Alexander Milne Calder, had sent a carved panel of "birds attacked by a snake" to be shown at the Centennial in 1876. Later he became famous with his huge statue of William Penn, which still stands atop City Hall in Philadelphia. Alexander Milne Calder's son, Alexander Stirling Calder, sent a few minor pieces to the World's Columbian in 1893 and some to the Buffalo Pan-American in 1901. He became famous when two of his largest works were displayed in the St. Louis fair of 1904 and his *Nations of the East* and *Nations of the West* at the Jewel City in 1915. Now, Stirling's son was mixing sculpture with water and music.

Another famous sculptor appeared at the World of Tomorrow, James Earle Fraser, whose *End of the Trail* had been popular in 1915. This time Fraser made a huge statue of George Washington as he had appeared for his inauguration. The statue, its profile thrown against the Perisphere, was most dramatic at night.

Children who were too small to walk all 370 blocks of the fair had their own Children's World to go to. Each child received a "passport" to a "Trip Around the World" on a miniature railway. The train stopped in various countries so the children could ride the burros in Mexico, sail on an Italian lake, drive small electric cars on an international highway. Mother Goose was out of favor for decorations—Children's World was filled with characters from cartoons, animals, radio pals, and Walt Disney's Mickey and Minnie Mouse.

Foot-weary older people rented the new battery-powered chairs. These had horns that played "East Side, West Side" instead of giving an ordinary toot.

Some people still loved riding in gondolas on the lake, but younger people rented the less romantic pedal boats. A grand tour of the fair with a guide, including dinner at one of the foreign pavilions and an evening performance, cost $5 for 5 hours.

The Aquacade had begun three years before at a fair in Cleveland and was so popular there that both 1939 fairs had the swimming ballet with beautiful girls, lots of flag-waving, and a curtain of colored water. Treasure Island's version had movie stars Esther Williams and Johnny "Tarzan" Weissmuller as its stars. World of Tomorrow had Eleanor Holm (former Olympic backstroke champion) and Buster Crabbe, another movie "Tarzan," with 500 hand-picked aquabelles and aquabeaux, the music of the Vincent Lopez orchestra, and plenty of action. The rainbow curtain sent 8,000 gallons of water 40 feet into the air to hide the changing of scenes.

Fairgoers who remembered the elegant displays of Czechoslovakian glass from other fairs and who had admired the happy,

Both fairs had the swimming ballet called the Aqua-cade

dancing people could not help feeling the war had at last touched them when they saw the Czech building. It was a brave, attractive modern design put together just as the country was falling into Nazi hands. In bold letters at the top were these words:

> After the tempest of wrath has passed,
> the rule of thy country will return to thee,
> O Czech people.

Next to it was the U.S.S.R. building, topped by a huge statue of a man holding a red star. In the building, fairgoers gasped with disbelief at a scene (made larger with mirrors) of the Mayakovsky Square subway station in Moscow. No one could imagine such beauty beneath the streets as the Russians showed. At the end of 1939, the Russians tore the building down and took their statue of "Big Joe" with them back to Russia.

The amusement zone at the World of Tomorrow had no special name—it was called "The Great White Way" because of the lights. All the shows were simply entertainment. Fair visitors of the past would have felt quite at home seeing the incubator babies, roller coasters, live monsters, midgets, assorted snakes, and "Nature's Mistakes" with freak animals.

The Russian building, topped by a worker holding the
red star, is beside the building of a doomed country

One unusual building was the "Crystal Palace of 1939." "See yesterday and today and the world of tomorrow," called the barker. The building was an exact copy, except for size, of the 1853 Crystal Palace, and inside were exhibits to show the changing styles and manners during the past hundred years. A theater showed all the popular entertainments from 1853 to 1892, including Tom Thumb, Jenny Lind, the Siamese twins, and "Cochetta," a female baritone singer. Another theater showed entertainment since 1893, including Sandow the strong man, Little Egypt and her educated muscles, and the famous painting of "Stella (Have You Seen Her?)."

The New York Zoological Society added to the strange and fantastic World of Tomorrow theme by showing the bathysphere in which Dr. William Beebe had descended a half mile into the ocean. Also shown were pictures of strange creatures found in the sea off New York harbor. And for the first time, many Americans saw a panda, an electric eel, and weird insects from tropical countries.

Fairgoers could take a trip through "Old New York" and meet famous people from the Gay Nineties. Shakespeare fans could go to "Merrie Olde England" and hear the Welsh Choral Singing and see a condensed version of *Romeo and Juliet*. A trip to Holland included a boat ride on the Zuider Zee. And Frank "Bring 'Em Back Alive" Buck's Jungleland was filled with exotic and unusual animals around a genuine jungle camp. Sun Valley's "Winter Wonderland" had a disappearing ice-skating rink, toboggans, ski jumping, and a 40-foot waterfall.

A scientifically accurate rocket ship ride through space took passengers to the planets and the moon, where they even had a view of the way the earth might look from there. Visitors who liked travel here on earth enjoyed "Victoria Falls," even though it was the same old concession where fairgoers at other fairs had walked up a curved ramp, past tropical rain forests, and through

The Transportation Show featured the role of the railroads in the nation's history and ended with the promise of better railroads to come

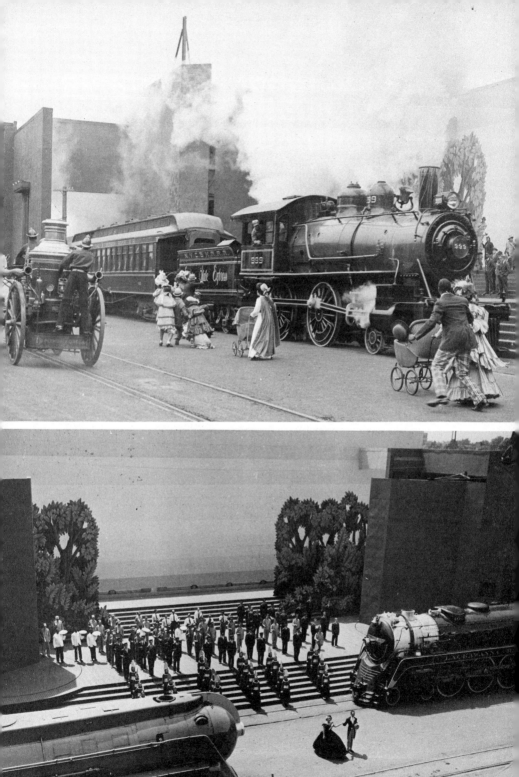

a door (in the Rhodesian jungle?) where they suddenly found themselves looking down into the ravine with Victoria Falls foaming over the cliffs.

A pageant of transportation featured all the changes that had come to the railroads since the year of the first United States fair. Real locomotives and railroad cars passed each other across a gigantic outdoor stage.

Before the summer of 1939 had ended, both fairs had planned to stay open for another year. It was a sad decision, because the world situation became worse. Treasure Island called its next year "Fun in the Forties" and the World of Tomorrow dredged up the hopeless theme "For Peace and Freedom." While neutral United States played at having fairs, the Nazis were moving into the cities of America's traditional allies—all but the British. Pavilions closed down as countries went to war. They took the hearts of both fairs with them when they left.

Few people even stood around to watch as the two fairs disappeared. Workers did their jobs, then went off to sign up for defense jobs.

In California, Treasure Island already belonged to Pan American Airways. But now the Navy needed the whole air base that Pan American had been sharing at Alameda. Immediately the big China Clippers and other commercial airplanes were to be moved to the island. Only a few buildings were left for the Pan American headquarters, including the two large airplane hangars. After the attack on Pearl Harbor, America declared war on two oceans. The Navy moved onto Treasure Island too and is still there today. A new airport was built south of San Francisco for commercial airliners, including Pan American.

In New York, the fairgrounds became Flushing Meadows Park and included five baseball diamonds, a swimming pool (the Aquacade), cricket and hockey fields, boccie courts, a pitch and putt golf course, a jogging course, a bicycle path, a marina, a zoo, and a good place to fish. The New York City Building was kept, with its indoor ice-skating rink, and the Parachute Jump was moved to Coney Island Amusement Park.

Almost the entire civilized world went to war shortly after the two fairs ended. Seventeen years passed between the end of the war and the next fair. The teen-agers who had visited the two fairs now had teen-age children of their own who were excited to see what a really big fair looked like. They had their first chance when the Century 21 Exposition opened in Seattle, Washington. There they rode on the country's first successful monorail and saw the sights from the revolving top of the Space Needle. Even the grown-ups were astonished at the new developments that had come since the last fair they had seen—the Polaroid camera, power steering, and puncture-sealing tires, 33⅓ rpm records, copy machines, digital computers, nuclear submarines, polio vaccine, and transistor radios.

8

New York World's Fair
1964–1965

A popular young President, John F. Kennedy, had been assassinated. The tragedy cast gloom over an entire winter. The war in Southeast Asia had been dragging along, and almost twenty-four thousand young Americans were in Vietnam. College students in California had begun rioting. Now the city that had begun America's fairs 111 years before was planning to hold a huge world's fair for two summers.

There was no special reason for having a fair—just a feeling that the time for one had come. Opening Day, April 22, was the 300th anniversary of the naming of New York by the British, who had not cared for "New Amsterdam," as the Dutch had called it. It was also the 15th anniversary of the United Nations in the city. The fair managers hoped that in some way the fair might bring peace to the world through better understanding between nations. But peace did not come. Before the fair ended, eight times as many Americans were sent to Vietnam, even though war had never been actually declared.

Since the last large fair in the East, jet planes had begun replacing propeller-driven airplanes. Scientists had discovered a definite link between smoking and cancer. Astronaut Gordon Cooper had orbited the earth 22 times in a space capsule. And the Gemini program (which some scientists believed could really put a man on the moon) was just about to begin.

Young people were enjoying the soul music of Aretha Franklin and folk music sung by Joan Baez and Peter, Paul, and Mary. By the time most teen-agers' parents had learned to live with the Beatles' music boosted by electronic instruments and amplifiers, their children's tastes had moved on to rock 'n' roll. Dancers stood as far apart as they had in 1853, since body contact was not needed to dance the twist, the monkey, and the frug. Radio was now mostly recordings and "telephone-in" shows, because the television set had become the most important article of furniture in the house.

The coming of another large fair still held enchantment for Americans. People cheerfully paid the $2 admission fee ($1 for

The Unisphere, built of stainless steel, was the largest globe of the world ever made

[ILLUSTRATION ON PRECEDING TWO PAGES]
The setting was the same—Flushing Meadows. But
the fair that opened in 1964 was very different

children) because almost everything inside the fair was free. They stood in hour-long waiting lines at every exhibit, spending the time getting acquainted with other people in line. Americans were no longer shy with each other. The country was almost two hundred years old, and by now its citizens had many experiences in common to help them get acquainted easily. Some compared notes on this fair and on the last New York fair in 1939. The setting was the same—Flushing Meadows. But where the Trylon and the Perisphere had stood 25 years ago, a new symbol rose.

The Unisphere, built of stainless steel, was the largest globe of the world ever made. Its builders had problems because the chunks of land masses are not evenly distributed over the globe, so the huge ball was unbalanced. The wind, pushing against the large pieces of land, threatened to shove the Unisphere off its pedestal. Engineers said it would have taken them ten years to design the Unisphere without the use of a computer. And they could not have built it without the help of Mohawk Indians, who had a talent for working in high, breezy places. To honor those Indians one of the small lights on the U.S. map on the Unisphere marked the site of a Mohawk Indian reservation on the St. Lawrence River.

Most people came to the fair in their own automobiles. Public transportation was dirty, uncomfortable, and not particularly cheap. Americans had become so used to driving their own cars everywhere that not many people even thought about getting to the fair any other way. The fair managers had provided huge parking lots. Someone figured out that if all the cars taking people to the fair had been parked in single file, they would form a traffic jam that would wrap around the world three times!

With fairgoers traveling by automobile, there was no longer the same need to stay near the fairgrounds, so many people found hotels and motels far away, driving to the fair every morning. "Motel" was a new word since the last New York fair—it meant "motor hotel." People who stayed in a motel could get easily from

Helicopters landed over the heads of diners at Top of the Fair

their cars straight to their rooms. That meant they no longer had to arrive at a hotel dressed neatly for the walk through the hotel lobby. They could even sneak in the family dog. Motels were important for families with children because they meant that traveling with children was easier and more relaxed than previously.

Almost six thousand children managed to get themselves lost the first year of the fair. Luckily for them, the fair police were prepared. Lost children were taken to the television studio, where they stepped in front of cameras. At the same moment, they appeared on 250 closed-circuit television screens which were scattered over the fairgrounds. Not one child was left "unfound."

"There will never be another fair like this," parents told their children (parents had been saying that to their children since 1853). But this fair had some signs of trouble never seen before. Foreign countries complained about the $6 per square foot of space they used during the two years of the fair. An American cleaning firm had been hired to clean the pavilions the first year, and foreign exhibitors found that wages paid to cleaning people in this country were as high as those paid to professors and engineers in some lands. The cost of having repairs made was equally alarming compared to what they would have cost at home. When a small sign blew off the British Pub one day, American workmen charged $92 (plus a free lunch) to hang it back up.

But visitors to the fair thought prices were very reasonable. At Morocco, they could eat shish kebab for $1 or have a traditional Indonesian thanksgiving meal for $6.50, including an evening's entertainment. Children especially liked the African Pavilion's Tree House, where they could feed Suzy the Giraffe and themselves for $4.50. Montana served buffalo steaks, Alaska had king crab, and Maryland had its own Chesapeake Bay crabs. The most exciting eating place may have been Top of the Fair, with helicop-

The architecture and lighting at this fair were purely Space Age

ters constantly taking off and landing on the roof. Snack bars listed fishwiches, chunks of sugarcane, egg foo yumburgers, kosher hot dogs, fresh pineapple on a stick, and banana fritters. The specialty of the Belgian Village was whipped cream and strawberries on a hot waffle.

The architecture of the fair was Space Age. Most people felt this style was all right for a fair, but surely such imaginative buildings would never be seen in their own cities. They were built of stainless steel, plastic, fiberglass, and other unlikely materials. One building had the world's largest suspension roof and another looked like a giant egg. Some were made like gigantic tents and others looked from a distance as if they were floating in space. Within the next ten years, every one of the new designs appeared in cities across the United States.

Instead of having huge palaces as in other fairs, the New York World's Fair was divided into five different areas—each with its large and small pavilions. Most of the industries were in the Industrial Area, although those industries connected with transportation had a separate Transportation Area of their own. In between the two were the International Area and the Federal/State Area. The only remnant left of the once-popular Midway was a small Lake Amusement Area. The delights of the old Midway had not been forgotten—they were scattered throughout the fairgrounds now, and many of them were free.

One of the longest waiting lines in the Industrial Area was at the egg-shaped IBM Pavilion with its "people wall." Musicians, perched on platforms high above the ground, played and sang for those waiting. Each time that five hundred people had filed into the seats—forming a solid wall of faces—the entire wall moved slowly up into the egg, where the audience watched a show about computers. Computers were a brand-new business idea to most people and would become a part of their everyday lives once the fair had ended. In 1939, the same company had displayed only some machines that canceled checks. Now the company was trying to educate the public to the fantastic things computers might do—such as translate foreign languages instantly, solve in minutes mathematical problems that until now had taken years to solve, and even help Sherlock Holmes solve some of his mysteries.

Computers seemed more exciting than color television at this fair. Most homes now had black-and-white television sets, and few people were surprised to see a color television. It was only a matter of time before the color sets became low enough in price for home use. All the fairgoers visited the RCA Pavilion, however, so they could see themselves on color television.

Fairgoers took a fifteen-minute armchair ride through the Bell Telephone Pavilion to hear about communication, from drumbeats in the jungle to the new Telstar satellite. At the end of summer, that satellite would be bringing the Olympic Games from Japan live into their own homes on their television sets. General Electric's pavilion showed a proposed model of controlled thermonuclear fusion which would take place at 20 million degrees Fahrenheit. The world's most powerful searchlight beam (12-billion candlepower) shone from the Tower of Light for hundreds of miles. The light was so bright that an ornithologist was kept on the premises to turn the light off in case it interfered with any migrating flocks of birds.

For children there were playgrounds like none ever seen before. The youngsters could clamber over statues or plastic formless forms. Some had peepholes through which a child could look to see a hidden duck, a giraffe, a man standing on his head. A company that made pens gave out the names and addresses of pen pals in foreign countries, selected carefully for each child by computer. Children climbed through a "nonsense machine" and found a robot they could operate by themselves. But the children's (and even their parents') favorite was a boat ride through a miniature world created by Walt Disney. Small animated children, animals, and birds all sang "It's a Small World" in various languages as the boat passed from one "country" to another on the ride.

The lifelike animations made by Walt Disney studios were a long way from the old robots that used to walk, talk, and smoke cigarettes in earlier fairs. Disney made dinosaurs, cavemen, and animals for several of the other exhibits at the fair. But one of his best creations was a startlingly lifelike Abraham Lincoln who spoke to audiences in the Illinois Pavilion. Lincoln sat down, stood up, and spoke, using as many facial expressions as a living person. He had more than 250,000 combinations of smiles, frowns, gestures, and movements—all programmed by computer.

Every fair seemed to have its star—at the New York World's Fair the star was Automation. It was not even necessary to push a button to start the hundreds of free shows at the fair. They were programmed to run by themselves. Stereophonic sound surrounded the audiences, making each person feel he was at the center of the stage. Superscreens often appeared above and all around the viewer. Movies were shown with dozens of projectors all working at the same time—all run by computers.

In the Transportation Area, young people who wanted to have a preview of life in the future headed for the Futurama of General Motors. Sitting in comfortable chairs, they rode along a ramp to see cars that rode on cushions of air instead of wheels, bubble-top cities to be built in hostile climates like Alaska's, an orbiting post office that sent picture mail around the world in seconds, foresters cutting down jungles with laser beams instead of saws, miners working under the ocean and on the moon, and farmers growing crops in the desert using desalted seawater. There was even something new for the billionaire who "had everything"—a competitive sport called weightless orbiting, and a resort hotel built at the bottom of the sea.

More long lines formed outside the Ford Motor Company's Magic Skyway, where fairgoers could climb into a brand-new Ford convertible for a ride through the story of transportation from dinosaurs to the City of Tomorrow. Instead of hearing the story through loudspeakers, the riders just tuned in on the car radio to hear it in one of four languages.

Children in the Transportation Area headed toward "Atomsville, U.S.A.," where they could run the remote-controlled manipulator that scientists used instead of their hands when working with radioactive materials. At another pavilion, they could hear the sound of stars, picked up by a radio telescope. Children ten years of age and older drove antique cars that looked like the ones their grandfathers might have bought in San Francisco's Jewel City. They were a little larger than half size and traveled at four miles an hour. The lifelike (and life-size) dinosaurs attracted more crowds of children. New Yorkers all remembered the day the dinosaurs came down the river. The huge models had been made in upstate New York. They were so large that the only way to get them to the fair was to float them on barges down the Hudson River. Thousands of people were caught in the traffic jam on the highway beside the river the day the monsters were moved downstream.

In the Federal/State Area, visitors poured into the New York

State Pavilion with its observation tower—the highest point at the fair. Actually it was only 226 feet high—not nearly so high as some fair high spots had been in other years. But the 1964 fair had a problem that had not bothered fair directors in 1939. Longer landing strips were needed for the jet planes arriving at and taking off from La Guardia airport nearby, and so the buildings had to be kept lower.

The time capsule that had been buried in 1939 was already "old-fashioned." Scientists wanted to bury another to show how much progress had been made in the past 25 years. Suggestions of what to include came from all over the United States. One group of campfire girls asked them to put in bubble gum, a yo-yo,

A favorite with blind children was Elsie the Borden cow

a talking doll, a twist record, and a hula hoop. Other people thought a wig, a bikini, false eyelashes, and hair dye would give a more appropriate idea of our civilization to people who would open this second capsule 5,000 years in the future. Here are the items finally decided on:

a bikini
a Polaroid camera
plastic wrap
an electric toothbrush
tranquilizers
a ball-point pen
a molecular block
a 50-star American flag
superconducting wire
a box of detergent
a transistor radio
fuel cells
an electronic watch
antibiotics
contact lenses
reels of microfilm
credit cards
a ruby laser rod
a ceramic magnet
filter cigarettes
a Beatles record
irradiated seeds
freeze-dried foods
a rechargeable
  flashlight

some synthetic fibers
a piece of the heat shield from
  Aurora 7
a copy of the Revised Standard
  Version of the Bible
a film history of the USS *Nautilus*
some fiber-reinforced material
a film identity badge
material from Echo II satellite
a computer memory unit
a pocket radiation monitor
graphite from first nuclear reactor
Vanguard satellite radio
  transmitter
a container for carbon-14
a piece of tektite
a piece of pure zirconium
some desalted Pacific Ocean water
birth-control pills
a pyroceramic baking dish
a plastic heart valve
a copy of the *Official Guide to
  New York World's Fair*
photographs of important events

Young people toured the Federal/State Area to find the Montana Pavilion where they could have their photographs taken riding a bucking pinto (stuffed) and walk through Cleopatra's throne room in the Hollywood Pavilion. They danced to jazz music in a special dance hall that served sodas and ice cream in New Orleans' Bourbon Street, walked through a West Virginia coal mine, and in Wisconsin gaped at the world's largest cheese, so big it could feed one mouse for 27 years.

The International Area attracted crowds just as foreign displays had always been able to do at American fairs. Only the Belgian Village, complete with cobblestone streets and authentic houses and shops, looked like the famous foreign villages of the past. But the fairgoers were able to get the flavor of almost a hundred foreign countries. They walked through the streets of Hong Kong, watched the African ballet dancers from Guinea, or the Flying Eagle of Papantla in Mexico, and visited art masterpieces from Spain that had never been out of that country before. One of the Dead Sea Scrolls (only recently discovered) was shown by Jordan in a replica of the very cave where it was found. Thailand had built another jeweled, golden Buddhist shrine which glittered and attracted admiring crowds. Children enjoyed Denmark's miniversion of its famous Tivoli Gardens where they could inspect a "For-

Glittering golden temples from Thailand stood out amid the Space Age buildings

A trip across the fairgrounds in the Swiss Sky Ride gave riders a bird's-eye view of the fair

bidden House," sail paper boats, and ride the dipsy doodle slide. The Swiss Sky Ride carried fairgoers in open buckets high above the crowd from one side of the fair to the other. And visitors of all religions went to the Vatican Pavilion to see Michelangelo's *Pietà*, the marble statue that looked like the finest porcelain against the blue drapes of the background.

The Lake Amusement Area had only a few of the shows left over from old fair Midways—puppets, wax museums, a circus, a long flume ride much like the old Shoot-the-Chutes, Indians, an aerial tower ride for a three-minute view of the fair, a ride in a Jaycopter that had once been used to train helicopter pilots, and a monorail that went nowhere. The amusements were mostly of the longer-lasting (and money-costing) type like a musical comedy, a Mississippi River showboat, a porpoise show, and an extravaganza in the amphitheater that had once held the popular Aquacade.

Now that American fairs were more than a hundred years old, people could begin to see in proper perspective the wonders that fairs brought with them. The old telephone that had made its quiet appearance in 1876 now came with touch tone dialing. There was a hint that in the near future there might be picture phones—where you could see the person you were talking to. "Family" telephone booths permitted everyone in a group to talk at the same time on the telephone without having to hold a mouthpiece. The old wireless had now become stereophonic radio without any of the static sounds that had once confused people into thinking other planets were trying to reach earth. The early Midway "trips to the moon" looked silly beside the real *Apollo* space capsule and the *X-15* research plane on exhibit. Silent movie films that had once fascinated fairgoers had turned into 3-dimensional Cinerama movies, films that surrounded the viewer with sound and multiple pictures.

The people who came to the fair had changed some, too. Some carried transistor radios so they could hear the baseball games and see the fair at the same time. They wore wristwatches, but now some were electric and some were self-winding. They carried credit cards in their wallets instead of money, and they wore clothes that were lightweight and comfortable. But in some ways they had not changed at all. The same spirit of good humor and enjoyment was still there.

Closing Day brought the feeling that there might not ever be another fair on such a grand scale. But people had always felt that way, and another fair in another city had always proved them wrong. The wreckers came as they always had. Every exhibitor had to agree to get rid of the building and clear the ground down to four feet deep. Then the area became the Flushing Meadows–Corona Park with over 1,200 acres which included a zoo, a sports arena, a heliport, a model-airplane field, an amphitheater, a marina, fountains and pools, a network of roadways, 14 baseball diamonds, 5 football and soccer fields, and an 18-hole golf course.

The Hall of Science stayed and was recently renewed. It contains a space station and orbiter, a mock nuclear power generator, a real satellite and a mock-up of the *Apollo* capsule, an amateur radio station, and many other worthwhile scientific exhibits. The Singer Bowl, used during the fair for many shows, including the Olympic trials in 1964, was refurbished. It is now the Louis Armstrong Stadium.

*The sculpture, Unisphere, and New York State Pavil-
ion in the background are still to be seen—but the
fair has gone, along with the people, flags flapping in
the breeze, the carefully tended gardens, and the
splashing water fountains*

The United States Pavilion, which had cost $14 million was
damaged by vandals. It was to have been torn down by the Federal Government, but they kept putting it off until the building
was almost wrecked. Finally it was taken down in 1977. Vandals
managed to ruin most of the fountains also. The New York City
building became the Queens Museum.

The geodesic dome of Buckminster Fuller is now an aviary for
the Queens Zoo on the old fairgrounds. The Underground House

is still there, but with the soil pushed over it so that only the builders know where it is. The Spanish Pavilion was taken to St. Louis, where it can be seen near the famous arch in that city. The Mormon Pavilion became a church on Long Island. The world's largest carillon at the Coca-Cola Pavilion was sent to Stone Mountain, Georgia.

The *Pietà* went back to Rome. There it was slightly damaged by a disturbed man who attacked it with a knife, but repairs were made soon afterward. The lampposts from the fair are now at the Orange County, N.Y., fairgrounds. The metal seats from one of the exhibits are in the Danbury, Connecticut, fairgrounds. The closed-circuit televisions were taken to various industrial plants to be used as "watchmen."

The General Electric Carousel of Progress went to Disneyland in California and remained there until 1973. Then it was moved to Disney World in Florida, where it is to be the center of a new show, modeled on the New York World's Fair of 1964–1965.

In the ten years after the fair, American families added a long list of marvels to their lives—most of them they had heard about for the first time at the New York World's Fair. There were electronic calculators in homes and schools, shirts and other garments that did not have to be ironed, machines that could copy whole pages from books at the flick of a switch, smaller "compact" cars thought to be just the right size for a family's second car, and ovens that cleaned themselves. The business world was changed drastically by computers and automation.

The biggest surprise to many people was learning that the Space Age was already here. Even before the fair ended, Astronaut Edward H. White had taken the first walk in space, and just after the fair closed, a team of astronauts proved that one spacecraft could join with another in space. In 1967, Congress got busy and passed an Outer Space Treaty to emphasize that no one nation could "own" outer space, build military bases out there, or make any tests that might destroy anything in space. Only four years after the New York World's Fair, the first man walked on the surface of the moon.

Fairs have taken Americans from building a better plow to designing vehicles to roam the planets during the course of 111 years. But fairs are not out of fashion yet. As long as America has problems, there will be fairs to help solve them. When everyone was worrying about ecology and harming the environment, there were two fairs to focus the world's attention on those problems and their solutions. In San Antonio, Texas, the Hemisfair of 1968 was all about the environment. In Spokane, Washington, the theme of the 1974 fair was "Man and His Environment."

Now U.S. leaders are worrying about energy. The planners of at least two large fairs are now building their "here today—gone tomorrow cities" on that theme. Expo '81 opens in Ontario, California, on May 1, 1981, to celebrate the United States at the start of its third century. The theme is "People to People—Pathways to Understanding," because the world's future may very well depend on how well the people of the world can communicate with one another.

The second fair now building is Energy Expo '82, a smaller fair than Expo '81, but with another very important theme. It is to be in Knoxville, Tennessee, near the energy center of Oak Ridge. The theme is "Energy Turns the World," and fairgoers will be seeing solar, fossil, geothermal, and nuclear energy put to new uses at a time when the older ways of getting energy are beginning to fail.

Bibliography

How does a person go to a fair years after the fair has been torn down and has disappeared? Here are some of the places where I found the fairs described in this book:

Art and Industry, as represented in the Exhibition at the Crystal Palace, New York 1853–4. From the *New York Tribune.* Rev. and ed. by Horace Greeley, 1853.

Augur, Helen, *Book of Fairs.* Harcourt, Brace and Company, Inc., 1939.

Authorized Visitors Guide to the Centennial Exposition. J. B. Lippincott Company, 1876.

Bancroft, Hubert Howe, *The Book of the Fair.* Crown Publishers, Bounty Books, 1894.

Barry, John D., *The City of Domes.* Published by John J. Newbegin, San Francisco, 1915.

Booth, M. L., *History of the City of New York.* 1867.

Brown, Dee, *The Year of the Century.* Charles Scribner's Sons, 1966.

Brown, H. C., *Book of Old New York.* 1913.

Centennial Exhibition, 1876, A. The National Museum of History and Technology, Smithsonian Institution, Washington, D.C., 1976.

Centennial Post, The. Newspaper, Smithsonian Institution, Washington, D.C., 1976.

Craven, Wayne, *Sculpture in America.* The Thomas Y. Crowell Company, 1968.

Curtis, William Elroy, *The Relics of Columbus.* William H. Losdermilk Co., Publishers, Washington, D.C., 1893.

Encyclopedia of American History, Bicentennial Edition, ed. by Richard B. Morris. Harper & Row, Publishers, Inc., 1976.

Exposition, The. Official Publication of Panama-Pacific International Exposition. Robert A. Reid, Official Publisher, Halleck Street, San Francisco, Calif., 1915.

Fair News. News magazine of the World's Fair Collectors Society, New York.

Fancy Fairs. Address to Philadelphia citizens, Philadelphia, 1834.

Fifty Years of Popular Mechanics, 1902–52, ed. by Edward L. Throm.

Simon & Schuster, Inc., 1952.

Francis, David R., *The Universal Exposition.* Louisiana Purchase Exposition Company, St. Louis, 1913.

Francis, J. W., *Old New York, or Reminiscenses of the past 60 years.* New York.

French, Yvonne, *The Great Exhibition.* London: The Harwill Press, 1852.

Going to the Fair. Sun Dial Press, 1939.

Gordon, Elizabeth, *What We Saw at Mme. World's Fair.* San Francisco: Samuel Levinson, Publisher, 1915.

Greatest of Expositions, The. Official Publication, published by Official Photographic Company of Louisiana Purchase Exposition, St. Louis, 1904.

Greeley, Horace, "Crystal Palace," from *New York Tribune,* 1853.

Haswell, Charles H., *Reminiscences of an Octogenarian of the City of New York.* Harper & Brothers, 1896.

Hemstreet, Charles, *Nooks and Corners of Old New York.* Charles Scribner's Sons, 1899.

Hilton, Suzanne, *The Way It Was—1876.* The Westminster Press, 1975.

Historical Societies of Philadelphia, New York, Chicago, Buffalo, St. Louis.

Jenks, Tudor, *The Century World's Fair Book for Boys and Girls, being the adventures of Harry and Philip and their tutor at the World's Columbian Exposition.* New York: The Century Company, 1893.

Kentucky Mechanics Institute, Louisville, 1854. Booklet.

Kimball, H. I., *Report of Director General on International Cotton Exposition.* D. Appleton & Co., 1882.

Langdon, William Chauncey, *Everyday Things in American Life 1776–1876.* Charles Scribner's Sons, 1949.

Letters about various world's fairs.

Macomber, Ben, *The Jewel City.* Published by John H. Williams, San Francisco, 1915.

Magazines of various fair years, including *American Heritage, Atlantic Monthly, Cosmopolitan, Current History, The Engineering Magazine, Frank Leslie's Illustrated Weekly, Harper's Monthly, Horizon, Look, Nation, National Geographic, Popular Mechanics, Putnam's Monthly, Scribner's, Time,* and *The World Today.*

Magic City, The. Portfolio of original photographic views of the Great World's Fair, from the Book Department of John Wanamaker. Published by H. S. Smith and C. R. Graham for Historical Publishing Co., Philadelphia, 1894.

Massachusetts Charitable Mechanic Association, 8th Exhibit. George C. Rand and Avery, Boston, Mass., 1856. Booklet.

Mattfeld, Julius, *Variety Music Cavalcade.* Prentice-Hall, Inc., 1971.

Mechanics Fair, San Francisco, 1857. Booklet.

Mechanics Institute, Washington, D.C., 1853. Booklet.

Moses, Frank, *American Metropolis,* 3 vols. 1897.

National Celebration, The. Report to Congress by the U.S. Centennial Commission. Government Printing Office, Washington, D.C., 1873.

New York Times. Issues for several years.

New York World's Fair. Illustrated by camera. Manhattan Post Card Publishing Co., N.Y.

Newspaper articles, pamphlets, and clippings found in scrapbooks.

Official catalogs, guidebooks, etc., for every fair except 1853.

Official Catalogue of Exhibits on the Midway Plaisance, Dept. M., Ethnology, ed. by the Department of Publicity and Promotion. W. B. Conkey Co., 1893.

Official Guide Book. Published by A Century of Progress, Administration Building, Chicago, 1933.

Official Guidebooks, San Francisco fair, 1939–1940.

Official Guide Book, World's Fair, N.Y., Rogers Kellogg, Stillson, Inc., 1940.

Official Guide to the Louisiana Purchase Exposition, compiled by M. J. Lowenstein. The Official Guide Company, St. Louis, 1904.

Official Handbook of the Panama-Pacific International Exposition, 1915. The Wahlgreen Company, Official Publishers, San Francisco, 1915.

Official Photographs of the Century of Progress Exposition, 1933.

Official Pictures of a Century of Progress. The Reuben H. Donnelley Corp., Chicago, 1933.

Official Souvenir Book, by the Editors of Time-Life Books. Time Inc., 1964.

Official Souvenir Book, New York World's Fair. Ed. by Frank Monaghan. Expo Publications Inc., 1939.

Official Story and Encyclopedia of a Century of Progress, compiled by Walter S. Franklin. Published by a Century of Progress, Administration Building, Chicago, 1933.

Official Views of Cotton States and International Exposition. C. B. Woodward Printing and Book Manufacturing Company, St. Louis, 1895.

Ohio Mechanics Institute, 1st Annual Fair, Cincinnati, Ohio, 1838. Booklet.

Poole, Mary, and Fletcher, William I., *Poole's Index to Periodical Literature.* H. W. Wilson Co.

Report of the Columbian Guard. World's Columbian Exhibition, Chicago, 1893.

San Francisco Chronicle. All newspapers of 1915 and 1939.

Scrapbooks on fairs at various historical societies.

Silliman, Prof. B., Jr., and Goodrich, C. R., Esq., *The World of Art and Industry.* Illustrated. G. P. Putnam's, 1854.

Stone, W. L., *History of New York City from discovery to 1868.*

Time Capsule of Cupaloy, The. Booklet.

Townsend, George, *People & Impressions of the World's Fair.* Chicago, 1893.

Truman, Major Ben C., *History of the World's Fair.* Philadelphia: J. W. Keeler & Co., 1893.

Views of the N.Y. World's Fair. Grinnell Lithographic Co., Inc., 1939.

Views of the N.Y. World's Fair. Long Island City: Quality Art Novelty Co., Inc., 1939.

Week at the Fair, A. Rand McNally & Company, 1893.

Wilson, R. R., *New York Old and New, Its Story,* 2d ed. N.d.

Witherspoon, Margaret Johanson, *Remembering the St. Louis World's Fair.* The Folkestone Press, 1973.

Index

About the Author

SUZANNE HILTON was born in Pittsburgh, Pennsylvania, but a family pattern of moving often into strange new neighborhoods started an inquisitiveness that has never been curbed. She attended nearly a dozen schools from California to Pennsylvania before attending Pennsylvania College for Women (now Chatham College) in Pittsburgh and graduating from Beaver College in Glenside, Pennsylvania.

During World War II, she used her knowledge of languages as a volunteer in the Foreign Inquiry Department of the American Red Cross. After the war, she married Warren M. Hilton, now an industrial and insurance engineer and Lt. Colonel, U.S. Army Reserve. With their son, Bruce, and daughter, Diana, the Hiltons traveled thousands of miles camping and sailing.

A busy free-lance writer, Suzanne Hilton has written eight books, seven of which have been Junior Literary Guild selections. She now lives in Jenkintown, Pennsylvania.